BURT FRANKLIN: BIBLIOGRAPHY & REFERENCE SERIES 331
Essays in Literature & Criticism 63

A Finding List of Political Poems Referring to English Affairs of the XIII. and XIV. Centuries

A Finding List of Political Poems Referring to English Affairs of the XIII. and XIV. Centuries

Sitteth alle stille   Ant herkneth to me

By LIVINGSTON CORSON

BURT FRANKLIN
NEW YORK

Published by BURT FRANKLIN
235 East 44th St., New York, N.Y. 10017
Originally Published: 1910
Reprinted: 1970
Printed in the U.S.A.

Library of Congress Card Catalog No.: 72-121221
Burt Franklin: Bibliography and Reference Series 331
Essays in Literature and Criticism 63

INTRODUCTION

I.

PURPOSE.

The projected volume, of which the following list is an abstract, has a two-fold purpose: (1) to provide a finding-list of political poems dealing with English affairs of the twelfth, thirteenth and fourteenth centuries, and (2) to publish the numerous scattered poems which remain as yet either unpublished or published only in miscellaneous and often rare collections of verse or in old historical works.

II.

PREDECESSORS.

The question is immediately suggested, what relation will this finding-list and body of hitherto unpublished poems bear to collections of political poems hitherto made, and to political poems incidentally printed elsewhere? The two standard collections of political verse are:

1. "The Political Songs of England, from the Reign of John to that of Edward II. Edited and translated by Thomas Wright, Esq., ... London. Printed for the Camden Society, ... MDCCCXXXIX." [Vol. VI]

2. "Political Poems and Songs relating to English History, composed during the period from the Accession of Edw. III. to that of Ric. III. Edited by Thomas Wright, Esq., . . . Published by the Authority of the Lords Commissioners of Her Majesty's Treasury, under the Direction of the Master of the Rolls. . . . . London . . . . 1859." [Vol. XIV].

Political poems are also incidentally published in some number in a few other works. Among these may be mentioned:

1. Wright and Halliwell's Reliquiae Antiquae.

2. Wright's two different volumes entitled Songs and Carols [Percy Society, XXIII and Warton Club, IV].

3. Furnwall's Political, Religious and Love Poems. [E.E.T.S., O·S. 15.]

4. Boeddeker's Altenglischen Dichtungen des Harleian Ms. 2253.

5. The Myvyrian Archaiology of Wales.
6. Histoire Litteraire de la France.
7. Rolls Series, the volumes of which, mostly mediaeval chronicles, have furnished more specimens of political verse than any of the above. For the full titles of the works cited see the list of abbreviations, p.x.; works containing only a few poems each are noted in the same place· Many works that promise a rich return yet remain to be searched before the projected volume shall appear. a.) County and family histories. b.) Works on German, Spanish and Italian literature corresponding to the H.L. de F. c.) The publications of the Historical Ms. Commissioners of Great Britain. d.) The numerous mediaeval mss., yet unpublished, in English libraries.

Thomas Wright, then, is the only editor who has made a considerable collection of English political poems as such and it is only with the poems of his two collections and those scattered elsewhere thru his numerous other works that the present list can profitably be compared.

III·

COMPARISON WITH WRIGHT'S COLLECTIONS.

1. Date. The following list of poems differs from Wright's two collections, first, as to the time covered by the poems noted in each. This list begins with eight poems relative to the death of Richard I in 1199 that are just too early to come within the scope of Wright's P. S. of E., which begins with John's reign. On the other hand this list includes no poem on events later than the accession of Henry IV in 1399, while Wright's P. P. & S. runs down to the recovery of the throne by Edward IV in 1471.

2. Number of poems. Wright's two collections so far from covering the field completely during the two hundred years here treated, do not include even all the political verse with which he was acquainted· In other of his works there are 38 poems on English conditions, in all likelihood written between 1199 and 1399, of the kind that he classifies as political and he must, from his antiquarian researches, have been perfectly familiar with the numerous scraps of political verse in the chronicles although he persistently ignores such poems. His two collections contain in all 127 poems, and for the years 1199-1399, 94 poems. The list which follows, although based on a decidedly incomplete examination of the

sources, adds to these 94 the titles of 169 hitherto uncollected. This is 131 more poems than the 132 Wright has published in or out of his two collections.

3. Length of poems. Many of the poems here first collected are short; the 121 of known length not in any of Wright's works contain 6848 lines, an average of 57 lines as against Wright's 132 poems of 18759, an average of 142 lines. Many of the poems in his two collections are of great length for pieces of occasional political verse, the 94 numbers that occur in the period 1199-1399 A. D. amounting to 16076 lines, an average of 171 lines. Nineteen of these poems are over 250 lines in length and amount to 11018 lines, an average of 580 lines. The 38 poems scattered thru other works edited by Mr. Wright average much shorter than those in the P. S. of E. and the P. P. & S. They amount to only 2683 lines, an average of 71 lines. Most of them are much shorter than this as two of them are of 958 and 311 lines and three more are over one hundred lines (128, 120, and 172 lines). With these five omitted the remaining 33 titles found in Wright's works outside his two great collections would average 30 lines. Omit the 18 of my titles (from works other than any of Wright's) of over 100 lines each and the remaining 103 average 14 lines.

4. Language. The present collection is also more inclusive than Wright's in regard to the languages represented. Disregarding even such broad dialectic distinctions as that between the Norman-French and the Provencal, Wright's poems are in three languages, Latin, French and English. The present list contains seven languages, the three found in Wright and Welsh, Irish, Norse and German. It is highly probable that a further search would soon reveal poems on mediaeval English political affairs in contemporary Spanish and Italian.

5. Importance. The additional poems here presented are so obviously of equal historical value with those in Wright's two collections that I shall cite but five out of many possible illustrations of this fact. Number 82, On The Murder of Hugh of Lincoln, strikingly reflects the anti-Jewish feeling of the XIII century (as, in a humorous way does No. 81), a matter which receives but scant incidental mention in Wright. This list, too, adds five poems on the popular feeling against the abuses of the church, (Nos. 245, 248, 250, 252, 253) besides a representative of a rarer class, poems in defence of the clergy, (No. 255).

The subject of Englishmen in the crusades, too, receives

no adequate mention in Wright's volumes.   Here, however, is a long poem, (No. 87) Dialogue between Henry de Lacy and Walter Biblesworth on the Crusade, which sheds much light on the contemporary feeling toward such expeditions. Here mention should be made of a poem found too late for insertion in the present list, The Assault on Massoura (**E.H.**, 64) whose 460 French lines celebrate the deeds of English and French heroes, notably William de Longespee in that disastrous assault in February, 1250.   This list also adds a number of such short continental invitations to English kings to go on crusade as Nos. 19 and 43.   Then, too, Wright has no treatment of England's continental relations, outside his poems on the English kings and their wars with France, comparable to the list here given which show us Englishmen involved not only in the Albigensian wars but in the more or less bloody squabbles for the shadowy honor of German Emperor (No. 47).   A glance at the sections of the list headed "Continental'' will at once reveal the scantiness of Wright's collections in this matter of illustrating Englishmen's activity and widespread reputation for bravery on the Continent, outside of the poems in which they boast of their own victories over the French·

Finally, for a   comprehensive survey of English conditions No. 157 will more than hold its own with any poem in Wright.

IV.

SUBJECT AND NATURE OF THE PROPOSED EDITION

Altho it would be premature to outline in advance of a fairly comprehensive examination of the sources the exact nature of the more complete edition of the scattered or unpublished political poems of which this list should show the need, yet an outline of some main features of its critical commentary may be of interest.

1. Definition of a Political Poem. Here the matter may be stated in question form: What features make a poem political or bar it from being a political poem?

a. Length. E. Goldsmid, who re-edited Wright's first collection (P.S. of E.) in the   Bibliotheca Curiosa in 1884, ridicules Wright for including pieces of such inordinate length as those mentioned above under the caption "political songs.'' Goldsmid's attack is an ill-natured quibble and his reasoning is specious.   Perhaps these long Latin poems were not sung but many a longer work has been. (Which of them approaches Beowulf in length?) Their length would certainly not prevent their being read, even read aloud, tho Goldsmid hints that it forbade their having circulation and influence.

    b. Language. It may be that the ordinary monk let alone the layman, could not understand Latin poems but who played the greatest part in England's affairs—such unlettered men or the scholarly churchmen, Stephen Langton and John Peckham? Even Goldsmid does not pretend that the numerous Anglo-Norman or French poems were rendered uninfluential by their language and no more were the Latin ones in an age when culture was largely classical.

    c. Positive criteria. After proving that neither great length nor being in a learned language would bar a poem from being classed as political, the proposed investigation might profitably search for essential qualities that every political poem should contain. Probably, as would also be the case with its treatment of the.negative.criteria noted above, the conclusions there reached would differ from the results sketched here but it now seems probable that three features would be selected by reason of their occurrence in practically every poem in this list.

    1) Contemporaneity, that is to say that a political poem, however antique may be its illustrations, bears on an evil or state of affairs existing at the time of writing.

    2) Wordly end. In distinction to the religious poem the political poem complains of worldly misfortunes not as signs of the triumph of evil but as lamentable per se and, when it has an expressed purpose, seeks to rouse men to better themselves in this world, not the next. And it is such direct comment on social or political states that is the main purpose of the political poem. Such material frequently occurs in other poems (cf. in Piers Plowman, for example, numerous passages of political satire) but they cannot be classed as political because their main purpose is to amuse, instruct or edify and not to rouse citizens to action, celebrate a victory, or eulogize a departed king and recount the events of the reign that made him beloved or hated.

    3) Definiteness of application. True political poems are not dateless stock maxims versified, but reflect evils of a particular time and country or seek to rouse to a particular action demanded by local circumstances. •Thus the numberless mediaeval poems that advise against marriage are not

political as they have no local or temporal setting and reflect no evils more characteristic of one country than of another. No. 201, however, to cite one example, was not only a direct outgrowth of English conditions under Edward III but must have roused many of the Kentish multitude who marched into London to be tricked into submission by Richard II. The purely local and particular character of such battlecries as Nos. 102 and 105 need but be mentioned.

Definition. If the discussion of this matter in the fuller edition should parallel this sketch, the definition of a political poem there presented would be: A contemporary poem bearing upon or illustrating by direct commént, not incidentally, political events or social conditions peculiar to some one country or period.

2. Extension of the Term Political Poem to Political Poems on English Affairs.

As noted above, the present list includes poems in seven languages. Language, then, has no weight in determining what poems shall be included under the term political poems on English affairs. But no poem is included in the list which does not deal with one of two classes of subject, a) social or political conditions or events in England, or b) the reputation or doings of Englishmen on the continent, either actual as No. 73, On the Murder of Henry of Almaine by Simon and Guy de Montfort (at Viterbo), or legendary, like No. 33, wherein the King of Ireland is used as a paraphrase for a man of great wealth·

3. Time Limitation.

The exclusion of even poems as nearly contemporary as those written in the XV Century, when they treat of XIII or XIV Century conditions, would call for some justification in the completed criticism. At present it is advisable merely to suggest the change in attitude inevitable with such upheavals as the Lollard Controversy and the Wars of the Roses, which would make many XV Century views of the XIV well-nigh as erroneous as that of any Elizabethan ballad on King John. But even if written with a full and unbiased grasp of the conditions of the preceding period, such a poem would have to be excluded as being plainly without possibility of influence on the time treated. True political poems, in the sense of the term defined above, not only flow from the emotions producd by the circumstances attending their writing, but show by their form and spirit the writer's wish to influence his audience—to move them to revolt with him, or join with him in deriding the corrupt, or share his joy in celebrating their hero's victory.

4. Classes of Political Poems.

An edition of the political poems of the XIII and XIV Centuries based on a thoro examination of the sources, would afford material for an instructive classification of such poems. The poems might be divided a.) by form, in to such classes e. g., as short martial lyrics, (Nos. 43, 112) epigrams, (Nos. 142, 212), long epics, often in Latin, (Nos. 119, 223,226), epitaphs, (Nos. 3, 12, 150), vernacular lyrics, (Nos. 22, 174), and the like. Here, perhaps, would be the best connection in which to trace the deviation of the distinctive metres of many abusive and humorous poems from parts of the Latin church service and serious or heroic poems in English. The poems might also be classified b.) by content, into satires, (Nos. 140, 251), praise or worship of popular heroes, (Nos. 141, 256—263), attacks on traitors or tyrants, (Nos. 16, 99, 143), reviews of reigns of lately dead kings (Nos. 191, 224), and numerous other groups. Each group would fall into several sub-divisions, as suggested by the sub-divisions of the group of poems on the church in the present list (pp. 7—8.) Certain themes also (against the taxes, against lawyers, the tax-collector keeps more than he gives to the king, etc.) that recur in several poems would call for full treatment and might, in some cases, demand an investigation of continental literature, as, for example, the satires on the church and the poems which boldly attack tyrants even tho reigning kings.

5. Relation of Form to Content.

Does the average attack on the church make use of a hymn-stanza or the like? A consideration of this question would naturally be followed by pointing out what the present investigation has made plain, that the songs in praise of popular heroes are often written in the service books as regular church offices. A full treatment of the many questions in this section would involve most fields of mediaeval prosody.

6. Necessary Exclusions.

The distinction between a political poem and a verse chronicle is not always so obvious as one would expect. Cf. No. 223, Gower's Tripartite Chronicle. This then, would call for treatment as well as such grounds of exclusion as would bar such a poem as Piers Plowman (its religious character, for one) and many of the lyrics of the period, e. g. "The Frere

and the Boy'' (where the humorous and story-telling qualities
outweigh the satire).

7. Conditions leading to Composition and under which
Poems were read.

One point made plain in this connection would be the
possibility of a long Latin poem, such as Goldsmid derides,
having a great influence thru being read aloud at a monastery
or university and so forming the ideas of some future church-
man-politician.

8· Evaluation of the Part Played in English Life by
the Poems of the several Classes.

9. Estimate of Their Historical Value To-Day.

10. Discussion of Mode of Arrangement.

The method used in the present list would not improbably
call for modification in the fuller edition. Here the poems
are divided, according to the time of the events treated, into
reigns; and the poems under each reign are divided according
to subject. The arrangement of the poems in each group is,
as far as possible, chronological, the date assigned to each being, when possible, that of writing, which is seldom known,
but oftener that of the events treated. Such occasional verse
is, however, nearly always contemporary. While this chronological arrangement (especially the separation into reigns)
may seem arbitrary, it has several points in its favor. a) It
follows Wright's arrangement, tho he does not attempt a
subject classification, and so facilitates cross-reference. b) It
facilitates reference to poems on an event whose date is known
and indicates at once if there are any poems specifically on
that event. c) It is largely suggested by the nature of the
poems themselves. Cf. the regularity with which the close of
each reign is marked by laments at the king's death or reviews
of its main events.

But this principle of chronological arrangement is in-
applicable to the poems on the church and those on popular
heroes. Attacks on the church vary little if any in the years
between 1199 and 1399, so only those are included under the
reign of writing that refer to specific events, such for instance as No. 30, On Simon's Election to the See of Norwich,
which attacks a particular instance of simony. But very few
references to particular crimes will be found in the poems se-
lected from both centuries and grouped as a class on pp. 7—8.
These contain attacks on the faults of the clergy—lust, avar-
ice, deceit, common to all European literatures before and

after the period covered by this list. In a word, the hastiest investigation of the matter will show that this group are a) not more closely connected with XIII Century events than with XIV; b) not characteristically English but part of a Europe-wide literature of abuse and as such deserving of separate treatment in their proper and greatly wider setting. All the above applies with equal force to the poems in praise or worship of popular heroes. Since the English wrote services in honor of their popular saints (see p. 45) for the services in honor of St. Thomas of Canterbury, and p. 46 for a hymn to Simon de Montfort) how much more must the Italians, French and Spanish have done so?

11. Indication of Additions to Wright's Collections.

The present list gives, besides the title, first line, date and number of lines in each poem, a source in which it can readily be found. Poems not included in either of Thomas Wright's collections (here noted as C. S. VI and P. P. & S.) are made prominent by having their source noted in blackface type, thus: **R.S.**, **H.L· de F.**, **R.** This is done even in the case of poems taken from Wright's other works which he does not include in his two collections of political poems, e. g., **R.A**. and **R.S**. XLVII.

NOTES AND ABBREVIATIONS

A.=Archaeologia; or Miscellaneous Tracts relating to Antiquity. Pub. by the Society of Antiquaries, London, 1770—·

A. L.=De Antiquis Legibus Liber. Cronica Maiorum et Vicecomitum Londoniarum et quedam, que contingebant Temporibus illis ab Anno MCLXXVIII°; ad Annum MCCLXXIV^m; Ed. by Thomas Stapleton for C.S., Vol. XXXIV. London, 1846.

A.S. & B.=Ancient Songs and Ballads, from the Reign of King Henry the Second to the Revolution. Collected by J. Ritson. London, 1829.

B.=Bards of The Gael and Gall, examples of the poetic literature of Erinn, ... George Sigerson, London, 1907.

C.=The Works of Geoffrey Chaucer, Globe Edition. Ed. by A. W. Pollock and others. London, 1903.

C.H.=The Cambridge History of English Literature, ed. by A. W. Ward and A. R. Waller. New York and London. 1907.

C.S.=Camden Society Publications. London, 1838—.

C.S. VI.=The Political Songs of England, from the reign of John to that of Edward II. Edited and translated by Thomas Wright, London; printed for the Camden Society, 1839.

Date given after a poem is that of composition. Where given without comment after a title from P.S. of E., or P.P. & S., it is on Wright's authority, and so occasionally based on scanty grounds. This list omits his dates in cases where the evidence is utterly insufficient but includes them, followed by (?), where they may be correct tho a possibility of error is evident from his data.

E.E.=Evan Evans, "Some Specimens of the Poetry of the Ancient Welsh Bards . . . . " Reprinted from Dodsley's edition of 1764. Llanidloes, Montgomery. (No date.)

E.E.T.S.=Early English Text Society publications. O.S.= Original Series.

E.H.=Excerpta Historica, or Illustrations of English History. Samuel Bentley, 1833.

F.=The New Chronicles of England and France, in two parts; by R. F., named by himself The Concordance of histories. . . . . . ed. by H. Ellis, London, 1811. [Fabyan's Chronicle.]

G.E.=George Ellis (1745—1815).

H.L. de F.=Histoire Litteraire de La France, Ouvrage commence par des Religieux Benedictins de la Congregation de Saint Maur, et continue par des Membres de l'Institut (Academie royale des Inscriptions et Belles-Lettres.) Paris.

H. of L.=Poems relative to Hugh of Lincoln, edited by J. O. Halliwell-Phillipps,in his Contributions to early English Literature derived chiefly from rare books and ancient inedited manuscripts from the fifteenth to the seventeenth century. London, 1849.

H. P.=James Orchard Halliwell-Phillips, (1820—1889).

Kreuzlied=A song to incite the person addressed to go on a crusade.

L. & S.=Essays on subjects connected with the Literature, Popular Superstitions and History of England in the Middle Ages. Thomas Wright. London, 1846.

M. A.=The Myvyrian Archaiology of Wales, ed. by Owen Jones and others. Denbigh, 1870.

Mackinnon=The History of Edward The Third (1327-1377). By James Mackinnon. London, 1900.

P. P. & S.=Political Poems and Songs, relating to English History, composed during the period from the Accession of Edw. III. to that of Ric. III. Edited by Thomas Wright. Rolls Series, Vol. 14, London, 1859.

P.R. & N.T.=Popular Rhymes and Nursery Tales: A sequel to the Nursery Rhymes of England. J. O. Halliwell-Phillipps. London, 1849.

P.S.=Percy Society Publications. 31 vols. London, 1840-1852.

P.S. of E, see C.S. VI.

R.=Joseph Ritson (1753—1803).

R. of C.=The Roll of Arms of the Princes, Barons and Knights who attended King Edward I. to the siege of Caerlaverock, in 1300. Ed. . . . . by Thomas Wright. London, 1864.

R.S.=The Chronicles and Memorials of Great Britain and Ireland during the Middle Ages. Published by the authority of Her Majesty's Treasury, under the direction of the Master of The Rolls. London, 1858—date. [Rolls Series·]

S. & C.=Songs and Carols, edited by Thomas Wright· (Note that he twice edited mss. under this title, first in 1847, Ms.   for the Percy Society [Vol. XXIII] and then in 1856 Ms. Sloane 2593 for the Warton Club.

Sirvente=A biting political satire in verse.

Spec.=Specimens of the Early English Poets. George Ellis.

S.S.=Scottish Songs. Ed. by Joseph Ritson, London, 1794. (See "R.")

T·S.=Thomas Stephens, "The Literature of the Kymry; . . . . . ". Llandovery, 1849.

T. W.=Thomas Wright (1810—1877).

W. & H.=Thomas Wright and J. O. Halliwell-Phillipps·

W.C.=Warton Club Publications, 4 vols. London, 1855-1856.

Z=Die Lieder Peires von Auvergne, kritisch herausgegeben mit Einleitung, Uebersetzung, Kommentar und Glossar von Rudolf Zenker * * * * * Erlangen, 1900.

[   ]=Supplied by the editor.

OUTLINE OF CONTENTS

(The number of lines noted as the total of each group of titles is, of course, not accurate in every instance. This is due to two causes: a) only a few lines of a poem may refer to English affairs, as is the case with Nos. 18 and 34, but the total number of lines in the poem is used in compiling the table. b) Often a group contains one or more poems whose length has not been ascertained, e.g. Nos. 39 and 86, in which cases the number of lines is reckoned as 0 in finding the total for the group.

The total number of titles and lines from 1199 to the end of each reign appears in parentheses at the right.)

JOHN. 1199—1216.

Group.		Titles.	Lines.
A.	On the Death of Richard I. (Nos. 1—8)..	8	51
B.	John and Magna Charta..................	0	0
C.	John and the Pope. (Nos. 9—11)........	3	417
D.	Elegiac Poems. (No. 12).............	1	8
E.	Poems on Miscellaneous Subjects. (Nos. 13—15)	3	55
F.	On the Continent. (Nos. 16—19)........	4	184

Total: 19 titles, 715 lines. (19   715)

HENRY III. 1216—1272.

A.	Establishment. (Nos. 20—21)..........	2	150
B.	Baron's War. (Nos. 22—27)..........	6	1435
C.	On the Church. (Nos. 28—31)..........	4	93
D.	On the Continent. (Nos. 32—47).......	16	504
E.	Wales. (Nos. 48—62)................	15	1026
F.	Ireland. (Nos. 63 and 64).............	2	499
G.	Scotland. (No. 65)...................	1	136
H.	Elegiac Poems. (Nos. 66—74)..........	9	38
I.	Poems on Miscellaneous Subjects. (Nos. 75—90)	16	897

Total: 71 titles, 4778 lines. (90   5493)

EDWARD I. 1272—1307.

Group.	Titles.	Lines.
A. England. (Nos. 91—97)	7	699
B. France. (Nos. 98 and 99)	2	76
C. Wales. (No. 100)	1	8
D. Scotland, (Nos. 101—120)	20	1973
E. Elegiac Poems. (Nos. 121—126)	6	214
F. On the Continent, (excluding France.) (No. 127)	1	136
G. Poems on Miscellaneous Subjects. (Nos. 128—138)	11	645
H. Ireland. (Nos. 139—141)	3	254

Total: 51 titles, 4005 lines. (141 9498)

EDWARD II. 1307—1327.

	Titles.	Lines.
A. Edward vs. the Barons. (Nos. 142—147)	6	186
B. Scotland. (Nos. 148 and 149)	2	118
C. Elegiac Poems. (Nos. 150 and 151)	2	10
D. Poems on Miscellaneous Subjects. (Nos. 152—158)	7	1137

Total: 17 titles, 1451 lines. (158 10949)

EDWARD III. 1327—1377.

	Titles.	Lines.
A. The French War. (Nos. 159—173)	15	2462
B. English Affairs	0	0
C. Scotch Wars. (Nos. 114—184)	11	709
D. Spanish Wars. (Nos. 185—187)	3	808
E. Elegiac Poems. (Nos. 188—191)	4	298
F. Poems on Miscellaneous Subjects. (Nos. 192—200)	9	81

Total: 42 titles, 4358 lines. (200 15307)

RICHARD II. 1377—1399.

	Titles.	Lines.
A. The Peasant Revolt. (Nos. 201—206)	6	231
B. Lollardry. (Nos. 207—210)	4	1000
C. Spain	0	0
D. Ireland	0	0
E. England. (Nos. 211—224)	14	2399

Group.	Titles.	Lines.
F. France. (No. 225).....................	1	56
G. Scotland. (Nos. 226 and 227)...........	2	562
H. Elegiac Poems. (No. 228)..............	1	4
I. Poems on Miscellaneous Subjects. (Nos. 229 and 241).........................	13	1151
J. Welcome to Henry IV. (Nos. 242 and 243.)	2	492

Total: 43 titles, 5895 lines. (243 21202)

THE CHURCH.

	Titles.	Lines.
A. Direct Attacks on the Corruption of the Regular Clergy. (Nos. 244—249)......	6	2653
B. Satirical Plans for a Monk's Paradise. (Nos. 250 and 251)..................	2	438
C. Attacks on Carelesness in Church Services. (Nos. 252 and 253)...........	2	5
D. Attacks on the Ecclesiastical Courts. (No. 254)	1	90
E. Defenses of the Church. (No. 255).......	1	560

Total: 12 titles, 3746 lines. (255 24948)

POPULAR HEROES.

	Titles.	Lines.
A. For Use in the Church Service. (Nos. 256—260)	5	115
B. Miscellaneous Poems. (Nos. 261—263)...	3	76

Total: 8 titles, 191 lines. (263 25139)

JOHN

A. ON THE DEATH OF RICHARD I.

1. "Prophecy" of the Death of Richard I. **R.S.** XXXVI, II, xviii & 71. Date, 2 ll.

Pro miraculo habetur apud multos quod per multum tempus ante obitum regis solebant puellae Normanicae canere in choris,

"In Lomizin sagitta fabricatur,
Qua tyrannus morti dabitur"

Sed mirum nobis videtur quare tyrannus pronostice dicebatur, qui princeps piisimus, ut aestimabamus, existebat. Revera, quod mirum dictu est, postremo ille telo occubuit quod in Limozin fabricatum est.

2. Richard Forgives his Slayer. **R.S.** XLII, 272-3. Event, 1199. 2 ll.

E auderein fist il venir devant ly cely ki lout plaee e ly dist: "Quel mal fis jeo unkes a tey, pur quei ma tu twe?" E il meintenant respondi: "Ws tuastes mon pere e mes ii. freres de vostre meyn, e ws voleit a donkes aver twe mey meimes; pernet donc quel vengance ki vus volez de mei, je ne faz force; kar jeo suffray volunters quel mort e quel peine ws me volez fere aver, partens ke tant mal avez fet el mund." E donc le rey comanda ke il fut deslie e dist aly: "Jeo te pardoyn ma mort." Mes le bacheler estut meintenant devant les pez le rey ki out le quer gros etut bandement mist avant la teste pur receivre la mort. E quant le rey out ceo veu il ly dist,

"Certes tu viveras, quel talen ki tu as;
[E] jammes ma mort ne comperas."

En tele manere fust il lesse aler tut quite. E le rey comanda ke hom ly dona cent souz de la moneye de Engletere. Mes un y out malveys de Braban Marchadeus ki fust ou le rey, ki le prist par la meyn e le tint; e quant le rey fust mort il lescorcha e pus pendi.

3. Epitaph on Richard the Crusader. **R.S.** XLIII, p. 336. Date of death, 1199. 4 ll.

Christe, tui calicis praedo fit praedo Calucis:
Aere brevi dejicis qui tulit aera crucis.
Hic Ricarde, jaces, sed mors si cederet armis,
Victa timore tui cederet arma tuis.

4. Expolits of Richard on his Crusade. **R.S.** XLIX, II, 252. Date of crusade, 1190-91.   6 ll.
(The likeness of 11. 1 and 2 to 11. 3 and 4 is an example of the frequent borrowing of scraps of verse by the chroniclers.)

Rex Ricarde jaces; sed si mors cederet armis,
Victa timore tui, cederet ipsa tuis.
Laus tibi prima fuit Siculi, Cyprus altera, Jope
Tertia; quarta dromo; quinta cavarna fuit.
Suppressi Siculi; Cyprus pessundata; Jope
Tenta; dromo mersa; capta cavarna fuit.

5. Four Epigrams on Richard. **R.S.** LI, IV, 84. Dates, probably c. 1199, soon after Richard's death.

$$2+4+6+8=20 \text{ ll.}$$

(Sometimes printed together in varying order.)

a. In hujus morte perimit formica Leonem.
Proh dolor, in tanto funere mundus obit!

b. Viris, avarita, scelus, enormisque libido,
Foeda fames, atrox elatio, caeca cupido
Annis regnarunt bis quinis: arcubalista
Arte, manu, telo, prostravit viribus ista.

c. Si genus et probitas metas transcendere mortis
Possent, intrassem non ego mortis iter
Stare putas hominem, cui mors ab origine finem
Nunciat et meus est, ingeminat, meus est?
Longa manus morti; mors fortior Hectore forti;
Expugnat homines oppida, mors homines.

d. Hujus debellare nequivit virtutem magnorum turba
    laborum
Cujus iter, gressus, obstacula nulla retardant.
Non strepitus, non ira maris, non vallis abyssus,
Non juga, non celsi praeceps audacia montis,
Asperitasque viae saxis callosa, nec ipsae
Limitis ambages, desertaque nescia gressus,
Non rabies venti, non imbribus ebria nubes,
Non tonitrus horrenda lues, non nubilius aer.

6. On Richard's Burial. **R.S.**   XLIII, 336.   Date of burial, 1199.   4 ll.

Viscera Cariolun, corpus Fons servat Ebraudi,
Et cor Rothomagum, magne Ricarde, tuum,
In tria dividitur unus, qui plus fuit uno,
Nec superest uni gratia tanto viro.

7. On Richard's Burial. **R.S.** XIII, 96. Date, 6+5=11 ll.

a. Achaluz cecidit rex, regni cardo, Ricardus;

Hiis ferus, hic humilis, hic agnus, hiis leopardus.
Casus erat lucis Chaluz: per saecula nomen
Non intellectum fuerat; sed nominis omen
Non patuit, res clausa fuit: sed luce cadente
Prodiit in lucem, pro casu lucis adeptae.

b. Pictavis exta ducis sepelit, tellusque Chalucis
Corpus dat claudi, sub marmore Fontis Ebraudi,
Neustria, tuque tegis cor inexpugnabile regis,
Sic loca per trina se sparsit tanta ruina,
Nec fuit hoc funus cui sufficeret locus unus.

8. On Richard's Burial (13 ll. variant of above with two new lines, 7. 8) **R.S.** XLI, VIII, 171.

Acalus cecidit rex, regni cardo, Ricardus, . . .
Prodiit in lucem per casum lucis ademptae
Anno milleno ducenteno minus uno
Ambrosii festo decessit ab orbe molesto.
Pictavis exta ducis sepelis rea terra Calucis;
Neustria tuque tegis cor inexpugnabile regis;   l. 10
Corpus das dandi sub marmore Fontis Ebrardi.
Sic loca per trina se sumpsit tanta ruina
Ejus vita brevis cunctis plangetur in aevis.

B. JOHN AND MAGNA CHARTA.

(The entire absence of any contemporary allusions in verse to this phase of John's reign is one of the most striking facts brought out by the present list. The signing of this "charter of liberties" could not have been regarded at the time, as the modern historian considers it, as the most noteworthy event of the reign. Nor were the "metricians" silent on this agitation because they regarded it as too important for rhyme. In this reign we have poems on such serious matters as the interdict (No. 10), and on the impending loss of the English possessions in France, (Nos. 16 and 17). Cf., too, the numerous poems arising out of the Barons' War under Henry III. (Nos. 22—27).

C. JOHN AND THE POPE.

9. Song on the Bishops, C.S. VI, p. 6. c. 1207.   162 ll.
　　Complange tui, Anglia,
10. On the Interdict. **R.S.** XLIV, III, 224. Event, 1228. 2 ll.
　　Cum igitur papa plures et pluries nuncios ad regem destinasset, et nihil proficiebant, prima die Lunae in Passione Domini, scilicet x kalendas Aprilis, [March 23] sub gen-

erali interdicto conclusum est regnum Anglicanum.   Unde
quidam ait versificator,
    "Mille ducentenis annis, octoque peractis,
    Tollitur Angligenis cultus et ordo sacer."
Infiscantur igitur omnia bona ecclisiae in Anglia. Rex
autem sibi timens, homagia . . . . . . obsides.
11.   Sirvente on Rome.   **H.L.de F.** XVIII, 654. 1226-1229.
                                                    253 ll.
(The lines quoted contain the only reference to England in
the extracts from this sirvente given in the H. L. de F.)
    Sirventes vuelh far
    En est son que m'agensa,. . .
    Roma enganairitz,
    Qu'etz de totz mals guitz
    E sims e razitz;
    Lo bon reys d'Anglaterra
    Fon per vos trahitz.

D. ELEGIAC POEMS.

12.   Two Epitaphs on John, **R.S.** LVIII, II, 669.
Date of death, 1216.   6+2=8 ll.
    a.   Hoc in sarcophago sepelitur regis imago,
    Qui moriens multum sedavit in orbe tumultum,
    Et cui connexa dum vixit probra manebant.
    Hunc mala post mortem timor est ne fata sequantur.
    Qui legis haec, metuens dum cernis te moriturum,
    Discite quid rerum pariat tibi meta dierum.
    b.   Anglia sicut adhuc sordet foltore Johannis,
    Sordida foedatur foedante Johanne gehenna.

E. POEMS ON MISCELLANEOUS SUBJECTS.

13.   Three Poems in Praise of Giraldus Cambrensis. **R.S.**
XXI, III, pp. 95 and 96. Events, 1199.   10+14+20=44 ll.
    a.   Optime sancte David, virtus quem celsa beavit,
    b.   Spes tua Roma tibi defecit teque reliquit;
    c.   Giraldus girans discurrit ad ardua spirans
14.   On Richard de Marisco.   **R.S.** CXI, I, 244. 1213-1214.
                                                    2+6=8 ll.
(The passage occurs after an account of events in 1213 and
immediately before an account of the death of the Abbott
of St. Alban's in 1214).
    a.   Eodemque tempore, cum Ricardus de Marisco,
Regis principalis consiliarius, exactor pecuniae inexora-

bilis, supra modum ipsum Abbatem stimulando artavit, ut supradictam, pecuniam festivanter persolveret de ipso quoque dixit, ipsum Ricardum et Regem reprobando,—
"Non erit Abimelech requies, regnante Saul, nec
Pax stabilis, donec desinat esse Doech."
    b. Epitaphium Ricardi de Marisco episcopi Dunelmensis editum a quodam monacho Dunelmensi. **R.S.** LVII, III, 112. Date of death, 1226.

Culmina qui cupitis,	laudes pompasque sititis,
Est sedata sitis,	si me pensare velitis.
Qui populos regitis,	memores super omnia sitis
Quod mors inmitis	non parcit honore potitis.
Vobis praepositis	similis fuerum, bene scitis
Quod sum vos eritis,	ad me currendo venitis.

15. On the Marriage of Lady Margaret Rivers to Faulkes. **R.S.** LVII, V. 323. Event, 1215. 3 ll.

Eodemque anno, sexto nonas Octobis, (October 2, 1252) obiit nobilis ac generosa domina Margareta, comitissa de Insula, cognomento de Ripariis, quondam uxor Falcasii cruentissimi proditoris. Copulabatur tamen eidem ignobili nobilis, pia impio, turpi speciosa, invita et coacta, tradente eam Johanne tiranno, qui nullum genus abhorruit facinoris perpetrandi. De qua copula ait satis eleganter;
"Lex connectit eos, amor et concordia lecti:
Sed lex qualis? Amor qualis? concordia qualis?
Lex exlex, amor exosus, concordia discors."

F. ON THE CONTINENT.

16. Sirvente on King John. C.S. VI, 3. 1204-1205. 52 ll.
    Quant vei lo temps renovellar,
17. Song on the Siege of Thouars. C.S., VI, 1. 1206. 32 ll.
    Mors est li siecles briemant.
18. Sirvente on Robert, Bishop of Clermont, **H.L. de F.** XVIII, 613. (Raynouard, Choix, IV, 258). 1212. 32 ll.
    Vergoigna aura breument nostre evesque cantaire, . . .
    Et ab deniers dels mortz alonga al rie sa guerra:
    Aitan l'azire dieus cum el aura Englaterra.
    Englaterra aura el ben e fai gran fellonia,
    Que lo reis l'a cregut de mais qu'el non avia;
    (The lines quoted contain the only reference to England in the poem).
19. Kreuzlied, Mentioning John's Peace with Otto and Philip II. **Z.** p. 147. After 1214 (?) 68 ll.
    Lo senher que formet lo tro . . . . . .

Al rei Felip et a'n Oto
et al rei Joan eisamen
laus que fasson accordamen   1.35
entr'els e segon lo perdo,
e servon a sancta Maria,
don sos fils pert la senhoria
de Suria del comte de
Sur tor al renhe d'Egipte.

HENRY III.

A. ESTABLISHMENT.

20. The Taking of Lincoln. C.S. VI, p. 19.
Event, 1217.   148 ll.
   Serpserat Angligenam rabies quadrangula gentum.
21. On Falcasius' Surrender. **R.S.** XIII, 151.
Event, 1224.   2 ll.
   Tandem capto castello, [Bedford], suspensi sunt inter
milites et servientes plusquam lxxx., et factus est exul Falco, dominus tunc illius castri, per judicium regni Angliae;
et quasi in momento idem Falcasius de divite pauperrimus
effectus, multis poterit et maxime nocentibus fiere in ex-
emplum; de quo quidam sic ait:
   "Perdidit in mense Falco tam fervidus ense
   Omine sub saevo quicquid quaesivit ab aevo."

B. BARONS' WAR.

22. Song against the King of Almaigne. C.S. VI, p. 69.
Event, 1264.   56 ll.
   Sitteth alle stille ant herkneth to me:
23. The Battle of Lewes. C.S. VI, p. 72. Event, 1264. 968 ll.
   Calamus velociter scribe sic scribentis,
24. The Song of the Barons. C.S. VI, p. 59. 1263(?)
(Beginning and end lost.)   Remain, 80 ll.
   M'es de Warenne ly bon quens,
25. Song upon the Divisions among the Barons. C.S. VI,
p. 121. Date, probably contemporary.   48 ll.
   Plange plorans, Anglia, plena jam dolore;
26. The Lament of Simon de Montfort. C.S. VI, p. 125.
Event, 1265.   54 ll.
   Chaunter m'estoit, mon cuer le voit, en un dure langage,
27. Deeds and Death of Simon de Montfort. **H.P.** in
C. S. XV, 139. Ante 1267.   229 ll
   Illos salvavit Mons Fortis quos superavit;

C. ON THE CHURCH.

28. The Song of the Church. C.S. VI, p. 42. 1256. 40 ll.
   Or est acumpli a men acient

29.   A Song Against the Bishops. C.S. VI, p. 44. 1256. 40 ll.
Licet aeger cum aegrotis.
(77.   Song on the Corruptions of the Time.   See under I.)
30.   On Simon's Election to the See of Norwich. R.S. I.
158.   Event 1259.   2 ll.
In that same tyme the monkis of Norwich chose to her
bishop a man that hite Simon, because he lent hem CCC
mark; of whech eleccion were mad these vers:
Trecente marce, Simon, si pontificent te,
Per numisma teres, fit Simon Simonis heres.
This is the English:-
Thre hundred mark, Simon, if thei make the bischop.
With mony thou tredis thi trace, so Simond Simon eyer
he was.
31.   On the Duty of Poverty among the Francisians. R.S.
IV, 25. 1225-50 or earlier.   11 ll.
In Thomas de Eccleston Liber de Adventu Minorum in
Angliam we read: Venit quoque Frater Henricus de Bur-
forde, qui cum adhuc novitius esset, et cantor Fratrum Paris-
ius, contra temptationes quas sustinuit versus istos in medi-
tatione composuit:
Qui Minor es, noli ridere, tibi quia soli
Convenit ut plores; jungas cum nomine mores.
Nomine tu Minor es, Minor actibus esto, labores
Perfer, et ingentem vincat patientia purgat
Si quicquam facis; est siquis te corripit? is est,
Qui te custodit; non te, sed quod facis, odit.
Quid tibi cum vili veste, cibo, quoque cubile?
Peccator certe, tu singula perdis aperte
Si mentitus eris factis quod veste fateris.
Umbra minoris erit, qui nulla re sua quaerit.

D. ON THE CONTINENT

32.   Allusion to Frederick II.'s Friendship for England.
H.L. de F. XIX, 472. Date uncertain. (Number of lines
not ascertained.)
Un sirventes vuelh far en aquest son de N Gui.
33.   Reference to "The King of Ireland." H.L. de F. XX,
576.   Date not ascertained.   38 ll.
(The lines quoted contain the only allusion to the British
Isles in the poem.)
Tot farai una demanda . . . . . .
No vuelh esser reis d'Irlanda,

Per tal qu'ieu emble ni tuelha
Castelh ni tor ni baranda,   l. 10.
Ni que l'autra gent cofonda.

34. Reference to Simon de Montfort's Fearlessness.
H.L. de F. 575. Date uncertain.   44 ll.
(The lines quoted contain the only allusion to England in the poem.)

Per folhs tenc Polles e Lombartz . . . . . .
Et aura 'l ops bos estandartz
E que fieira mielhs que Rotlans,   l. 10.
E que sapcha mais que Raynartz,
Et aia mais que Corbarans:
Ettema meyns mort
Qu' el coms de Montfort
Qui vol qu' a barrey
Lo mons li sopley.

35. A Sirvente on the Foes of Toulouse. **H.L. de F.**
XVIII, 554. 1224-1226. (Number of lines not ascertained.)

El nom de dieu qu' es paire omnipotens . . . . . .
Fas sirventes e prec li qu' el m' ampar . . . . . .

36. A Sirvente on Richard of Cornwall's Expedition into
Angou. **H.L. de F.** XX, 598. c. 1226.   46 ll.

Sendatz vermelhs, endis e ros,

37. A Sirvente against King Henry. C.S. VI, 36. **H.L. de F.**
XVIII, 667. c. 1229.   44 ll.

Ja no vuelh do ni esmenda.

38. A Sirvente against Henry III. of England and James I.
of Aragon. **H.L. de F.** XVIII, 666. c. 1229.   48 ll.

En talent ae q'un serventes encoc

39. A Sirvente on Three False Friends of Toulouse.
H.L. de F. 454. 1229. (Number of lines not ascertained.)

The H.L. de F. notes as source the "Ms. dit de Caumont,
piece 250" and refers to no printed edition. "Un autre sirvente parut dans la meme annce, [1229] a l'occasion du
traite de paix signe a Paris le 12 avril, entre le comte de
Toulouse et le roi Louis IX, par lequel Raymond VII fut
depouille de la plus grande partie de ses Etats. Le fidele et
genereux poete (Sordel) ne felicite ni n'accuse Raymond;
mais il attaque trois princes qu'il ne nomme point, et entre
lesquels sans donte est le roi d'Angleterre. Il leur reproche
de manquer d'honneur, de se laisser ravis leurs propres
terres, au lieu de secourir leur allie."

40. A "Complaint" on the Death of Blacas. **H.L. de F.**
XIX, 460. Date of death, 1229.   44 ll.

(This passage, wherein Sordel recommends certain cowards, including the King of England, to eat of Blacas' heart to become brave, is the only allusion to England in the poem.)

Planher vuelh Blacatz EN aquest leugier so, ...
Del rey engles me platz, quar es pauc coratjos,
Que manje pro del cor, pueys er valens e bos,
E cobrara la terra, per que viu de pretz blos,
Que 'l tol lo reys de Fransa, quar lo sap naulhos. 1.20.

41. Sirvente exhorting Henry III. to regain his Heritage. **H.L. de F.** XIX, 485. Date not ascertained. (Number of lines not ascertained.)

(The lines quoted are the only reference to England in the extracts in the H. L. de F.)

Era pueis . . . . . .
Lo reis engles cug qu' a 'l sanglut,   1. ?
Car tan lo ve hom estar mut
De demandar sas eretatz . . . .
Degra si menar dans totz latz
Coredors e cavals armatz
Tro cobres sas possessios . . . .
E' l flacs reis cui es Aragos.

42. A Sirvente calling together the Allies of Raymond VII. **H.L. de F.**, XIX, 489. 1242.   50 ll.

Belh m' es quan d' armas aug refrim.

43. An Invitation to Henry III. to join St. Louis' Crusade. de F. XIX, 562. c. 1248. (Number of lines not ascertained.)

Si mos chanz fos de joi ni de solatz.

44. A Sirvente against King Henry. C.S. VI, 39. (H.L. de F. XVIII, 669.) c. 1250.   52 ll.

D'un sirventes m' es grands volontatz preza.

45. Two Sirventes on the Aspirants to the Empire. **H.L. de F.** XIX, 554. c. 1263. (Number of lines not ascertained.) (These of course allude to Richard of Cornwall. Cf. No. 47.)

a. Ar es ben dretz
b. Ar es dretz qu'ieu chant e parlle.

46. Song of The Peace With England. C.S. VI, p. 63. Event, 1264.   88 ll.

Or vint la tens de May, que ce ros parrina.

47. Richard of Cornwall's War to Secure the Empire. **H.L. de F.** XXI, 442. Event, 1269.   50 ll.

Gens sine capite mag keinen Rath geschaffen.
Imperium vacat capite; so handt kein Hopt die Pfaffen.

E. WALES.

(The Myvyrian Archaiology of Wales contains, pp. 140-
282, an immense mass of verse supposed to have been written
between 1066 and 1282.   The following poems which contain
references to England are representative only of the few
Welsh poems that have been translated and are in no way in-
dicative of the great frequency of Welsh allusions to their
hereditary enemies. On this point the following letter is of
interest: "University College of N. Wales, Bangor, Nov. 9,
1909. My dear Sir: The so-called 'Gogynfeirdd' or Semi-
Primitive Bards, who wrote from 1066 to 1282 and whose
work is to be found in the Myvyrian Archaiology, pp. 140-283,
of the one volume or Denbigh edition, are full of political
allusions. In my forthcoming History of Wales, I am only
able to make a slight use of this very extensive material and
I have a senior student here who is making the topic one of
special study for the M. A. degree. As to allusions to the
English, you may take it that they are to be found in almost
every poem: 'Saeson' (i. e. Saxons) and 'Eingl' (Angles)
are the regular foes whom it is the glory of every subject of
barbaric eulogy to have fought and overcome. To pick out
the allusions would be a heavy task and scarcely a lighter
would it be to make a list of the poems containing them. Re-
gretting that I cannot give you more substantial assistance I
am Yours faithfully, John Edward Lloyd.")

48. Conciliatory Address to Rhys Gryg. **M.A.** p. 257, 1.
Lllyma Kygoryon Dadolwch. Ante 1250.   40 ll.

  Pa gessidy ui uodrydaf kreugar.

49. XIV and XVII Hoianau. **M.A.** p. 107, 1. Date not
ascertained.   16 ll.
Expulsion of Saxons by Kynan and Cadwaladr.

(Reference to the longed-for return of the ancient national
heroes who were to free Wales from the invaders.)

  a.   Oian a parchellan andaw de yn awr
  b.   Oian a pharchellan neud blodau drain
  Hear O little pig! listen to me now;
When the men of Gwynedd lay down their work,
There will be a sharp conflict—horns will be sounded,
Armour will be broken by sharp missiles;
When Normans come over the broad lake,
There will be an opposing of armies,
Britain will be subjected to gentle squires,
And there will be an atonement for the faults of London.

I will prophesy that two rightful princes
Will produce tranquillity from Heaven to earth,
Kynan and the especial Cadwaladr of Cambria;
Whole worlds will watch their counsels,
Reforming the land, checking the flow of blood,
And abolishing armies and theft;
And from that time forth, we shall be freed from all our
    ills,
And from the prevalence of generosity, none shall
    want. (T. S. 262.)
50. XVIII, XIX, and XX Hoianau. **M.A.** p. 107, r.
Date not ascertained. The Expulsion of the Saxons. 27 ll.
    a. Oian a parchellan mawr eryssi
    b. Oian a parchellan mor enrhyfedd
    c. Oian a parchellan andaw di yr eilon.
51. XXV Hoianau. Date so uncertain that the reference
may be to another English king. Prophecy alluding to
Henry (III?) **M.A.** p. 108, 1.   8 ll.
    Oian a pharcellan a phorchell ryni.
52. An Ode to Gruffud ap Llywelyn. **M.A.** p. 266, 1. Ante
1270, the date of the author's death, (T. S.)   30 ll.
    Arddwyreafy hael hwylglod ellwg
53. Englynion to Owen the Red. **M.A.** p. 266, 1. Ante 1260.
                                                     32 ll.
    Gwynet kein reuet cann rad nyth arllut.
54. Against Owain ap Gruffyd's Imprisonment. **M.A.** p.
267. Ante 1280.   38 ll.
    Gwr yssyt yn twr yn hirwesti
55. An Ode to Llywelyn ab Iorwerth. **M.A.**.p. 217, 1. Ante
1240, the date of Llywelyn's death.   46 ll.
    Gwr a wnaeth llewych o'r gorllewin.
He who created the glorious sun, and that cold pale
luminary the moon, grant that I attain the heights of poetry,
and be inspired with the genius of Myrddin[1]; that I may ex-
tol the praise of heroes, like Aneurin, in the day he sung his
celebrated Gododin; that I may set forth the happiness of
the inhabitants of Venedotia, the noble and prosperous prince
of Gwynedd, the stay and prop of his fair and pleasant
country. He is manly and heroic in the battle, his fame over-
spreadeth the country about the mountain of Breiddin.[2]

---

1. There were two Myrddins, or Merlins, as they are wrongly
written by the English, viz: Myrddin Emrys and Myrddin Wyllt;
the last was a noted poet, and there is a poem of his extant, entitled
Avallennau, or the Appleshire. (E. E.)

2. Craig Breiddin is a high hill in Montgomeryshire. (E. E.)

Since God created the first man, there never was his equal in the front of battle. Llewelyn the generous, of the race of princes, has struck terror and astonishment in the heart of kings. When he strove for superiority with Loegria's king, when he was wasting the country of Erbin, his troops were valiant and numerous. Great was the contusion when the shout was given, his sword was bathed in blood; proud were his nobles to see his army; when they heard the clashing of swords, then was felt the agony of wounds. — — — — — Many were the gashes in the conflict of war. Great was the confusion of the Saxons about the ditch of Knocking. The sword was broke in the hand of the warrior. Heads were covered with wounds, and the flood of human gore gushed in streams down the knees.

Llewelyn's empire is wide extended, he is renowned as far as Porth Ysgewin. Constantine was not his equal in undergoing hardships. Had I arrived to the height of prophecy, and the great gift of ancient poesy, I could not relate his prowess in action; no, Taliesin himself was unequal to the task. Before he finishes his course in this world, after he has lived a long life on earth, ere he goes to the deep and bone-bestrewed grave, ere the green herb grows over his tomb, may He that turned the water into wine, grant that he may have the Almighty's protection, and that for every sin, with which he hath been stained, he may receive remission. May Llewelyn, the noble and generous, never be confounded or ashamed when he arrives at that period, and may he be under the protection of the saints.'' (E. E., 18.)

56. To Llewelyn The Great. **M.A.** p. 225, r. Ante 1240. (See No. 55.)   141 ll.
    Kynarch om naf om neuawl Arglwyt.

57. Y Canu Bychan (The Little Song), Minor Ode to Llewelyn vab Yoreurth. **M.A.** p. 214, r. Ante 1240.   60 ll.
    Cyuarchaf ym ren cyuarchuawr awen

58. To Llywelyn ap Ioruerth. **M.A.** p. 210, r. Ante 1240.   206 ll.
    Crist creawdyr llywyawdyr llu daear

59. The Contention with the Poetasters. **M.A.** p. 258, r. Ante 1250.   42 ll.
    Arglwydd nef a llawr mawr a ryved
    Only one line in the poem refers to England. The pasasge in the translation containing it (T.S., p. 169) follows:
    Llywelyn, the glorious long sworded lion of war,
    Whose fame is known in distant parts,

Will not give false judgment; he will speak firmly,
He is one whose name will be popularly known,
One who owns the taxes of the port of London,
The worthless land of Britain and its residences, ...
60. An Ode to Llywelyn ap Grufudd. **M.A.** p . 239, l.
c. 1270. (T.S.) 156 ll.
Kynarchaf y dduw dawn ornolet
61. To Llewelyn ap Grufudd. **M.A.** p. 223, r. Ante 1240.
(T.S.) (?) 136 ll.
Traethws fy nhafawd
62. The Song of the Welsh. C. S. p. 56. Date un-
known. 48 ll.
Trucidare Saxones soliti Cambrenses.

F. IRELAND.

63. The Exiled Head. **B.** I, 207. Event, 1260. 280 ll.
Death of my heart! Is the head of Brian
64. On Erecting the Walls of New Ross. **A.** XXII, 307.
Event, 1265. 219 ll.

G. SCOTLAND.

65. Sixteen poems on King Hacon's Raid. **R.S.** LXXXVIII,
II, 333-350. 1263.
15 poems of 8 ll. each plus 1 poem of 16 ll.=136 ll.
Leysti lang-rastar
With well-walled hulls. (LXXXVIII, IV, 345-363)

H. ELEGIAC POEMS.

66. On Simon de Montfort, Sr. **R.S.** XIII, 130. Date of
death, 1217. 2 ll.
Dantur iidem fato, casuque cadunt iterato,
Simone Sublato, Mars, Parisque, Cato.
67. On William Marshal, Third Earl of Pembroke. **R.S.**
XIII, 130. Date of death, 1218. 2 ll.
Sum quem Saturnum sibi sensit Hybernia; Solem
Anglia; Mercurium Normannia; Gallia Martem.
68. On William de Longespee, Third Earl of Salisbury.**R.S.**
LVIII, III, 105. Date of death, 1226. 2 ll.
Flos comitum, Willelmus obit, stirps regia, longus
Ensis vaginam caepit habere brevem.
69. On Stephen Langton. **R.S.** XXXVI, II, 304. Date of
death, 1227. 4 ll.
Praesul virtutis Stephanus documenta salutis
Vivens multa dedit, moriens a morte recedit.

Forma gregis clerique decus, vitae speculator
Et speculum, Christique fuit devotus amator.
70. On William Marshal, Fourth Earl of Pembroke, **R.S.**
XXXVI, II, 309.   Date of death, 1231.   2 ll.
Militis istius mortem dolet Anglia; ridet
Wallia, viventis bella minasque timens.
71. On Richard Marshal, **R.S.** XXXVI, II, 315.   Date of
death, 1234.   8 ll.
These verses follow a detailed and eulogistic account of Rich-
ard Marshall's last days and death and Henry III.'s conse-
quent sorrow. There is no allusion to them in the prose text
of the Annales de Waverleia.
Livor edax, morum subversio, fax vitiorum
Vitricus Anglorum, rapuit solamen eorum.
Principis absque pare, gens livida mentis avarae
Praesumpsit clarae decus indolis anticipare.
Anglia, plange Marescallum, plangens lachrymare.
Causa subest, quare; quia pro te planxit amare.
Virtus militae, patriae protectio, gentis
Fraude ruit propriae. Misere Deus morientis. Amen.
72. On Edmund, Archbishop of Canterbury. **R.S.** XXXVI,
II, 327.   Date of death, 1240.   3 ll.
Beatus Aedmundus archiepiscopus Cantuariae, plenus
virtutibus et sanctitate, migravit ab hoc saeculo, xvi. kal. De-
cembris, et apud Pontiniacum sepultus est. Cujus merita
miracula testantur.
Hic erat Edmundus anima cum corpore mundus,
Quem non immundus poterat pervertere mundus
Anglorum genti faveas, Edmunde, petenti.
73. On the Murder of Henry of Almaine by Simon and
Guy de Montfort. **R.S.** XCIV, III, 22.   Event, 1270.   12 ll.
Regis Teutonici Ricardi clara propago
74. On Henry III. **F.** p. 369.   Date of death, 1272.   3 ll.
Tertius Henricus iacet hic, pietatis amicus:
Ecclesiam strauit istam quam post renouauit.
Reddat ei munus qui regnat trinus et unus.

I. POEMS ON MISCELLANEOUS SUBJECTS.

75. Song upon the Tailors. C.S. VI., 51.   Date uncertain.
                                                      90 ll.
Ego dixi, dii estis;
76. A Song on the Times. C.S. VI., 46.   Date uncertain.   88 ll.
Mundi libet vitia cunctis exarare;

77. Song on the Corruptions of the Times. C.S. VI, p. 17.
Date not ascertained.   160 ll.
     Quam sit lata scelerum et quam longa tela.

78. Epigram on Richard, Earl of Cornwall. **H.P.** in C.S.
XV, 112, n. c. 1258. (H.P.)   2 ll.
     The high price of provisions, however, according to
Matthew Paris, was not so much owing to scarcity, as to the
immense sums of money that the Earl of Cornwall had taken
out of the country; Paris, p. 958, [Wats ed. (?); but see
Chronica Majora, R.S. LVII., 673 and 710.] and Tyrrell, ii,
(977.) This Earl's immense riches caused the following
epigram:
     "Nummus ait, pro me
     Nubit Cornubiae Romae."

79. On the King's Changing his Seal. **R.S.** XIII, 219.
Event, 1259.   4 ll.
     The preceding paragraph in the Chronica Johannis de
Oxendes tells how Henry III resigned most of the English
continental possessions, except Aquitaine, to France.
Then follows, apparently without connection, this paragraph: Eodem tempore rex Angliae mutavit sigillum suum;
pro gladio sceptrum. Unde quidam sic.
     Est M.c.bis. l. ix. utinam concordia felix
     Andegavis, Pictavis, Neustria de gente relicta
     Anglorum cedunt tibi France, sigilla mutantur,
     Nomina tolluntur, fugit ensis, sceptra geruntur.

80. On the Taking of Damietta. **R.S.** XXXVI, I. 64.
Event, 1218.   2 ll.
     Vicesima ecclesiarum de tribus annis praecedentibus
datur in succursum Terrae Sanctae capta est civitas
Damietae a Christianis, nonis Novembris, non virtute hominum, sed sola potentia Dei:
     Anno sub nono decimo et mille ducentis
     Capta est celebris nonis Damieta Decembris.

81. The Jew of Tewkesbury. **R.S.** XLI, VIII, 246.
Event, 1259.   4 ll.
     Circa illud tempus apud Teoksbury quidam Judaeus per
diem Sabbati cecidit in latrinam, nec permisit se extrahi ob
reverentiam sui Sabbati, Sed Ricardus de Clara comes Glov-
erniae non permisit eum extrahi die Dominica ob reverentiam sui Sabbati et sic mortuus est.

     a. Dum Purgat ventrem Salmon Judaeus olentem,
     In foveam cecidit; "Hodie non abstrar," inquit.

Refertur comiti: comes subridit et inquit,
"Sabbata nostra quidem Salmon servabit ibidem."
b. Variant of above. R.S. XLI, VIII, 246, note 9. 2 ll.
De cujus obitu quidam metricus sic cecinit:
Sabbata sancta colo, de stecore surgere nolo;
Sabbata nostra quidem dum sunt remanebis ibidem."

82. On the Murder of Hugh of Lincoln. H.P., H. of L.
No. 1. Event, 1255. (Halliwell-Phillips)   368 ll.
Ore vez un bel chancon

83. Characteristics of Different Nations. R.A. I, 5. Date not
given.   9 ll.
Italici quae non sacra sunt et quae sacra vendunt;
Allobrogas de perfidia cuncti reprehendunt;
Teuthonici vix Catholici, nullius amici;
Gens, tibi, Flandrena, cibus est et potus avena;
Gens Normannigena fragili nutritur avena;
Subdola, ventosa, mendax, levis, invidiosa;
Vincere mos est Francigenis, nec sponte nocere;
Prodere dos Normannigenis belloque pavere;
Alvernus cantat, Brito notat, Anglia potat.

84. The Coming of Antichrist. R.S. LVII, VI, 80.
Events, 1242.   3 ll.
After an account of the ravages by the Tartars invading
Hungary in 1242 the Chronica Majora of Matthew Paris adds
this paragraph: His quoque temporibus propter terribiles
rumores hujusmodi eelebriter hi versus, Antichristi adventum
nuntiantes, recitabantur:
"Cum fuerint anni transacti mille ducenti,
Et quinquaginta, post partum Virginis Almae,
Tunc Antichrist nascetur daemone plenus."

85. On The Repentant Horse Thieves. R.S. XCVI, 11, 362
Event, 1267.   5 ll.
Anno Domini MCCLXVIJ. tempore discordiae inter
regem Henricum et barones Anglise, licet in conspectu baron-
um pretiosa valde fuerat libertas Sancti Edmundi, quidam
tamen ribaldi, de munitione Eliensi egredientes, equos quorun-
dam virorum qui in secretioribus locis curiae beati martyris
Edmundi occultabantur per medium infirmariae deducentes
in insulam Eliensem secum duxerunt. Quos cum quidam
monachus ejusdem loci insequeretur, magnatibus insulanis
rem gestam luculenter exposuit; tandem, dictis insulanis
sententiantibus, dicti ribaldi dolentes et poenitentes cum
dictis equis arbitrio dicti monachi committebantur. Quos
videlicet equos, cum ad altare Sancti Edmundi devotissime

reduxissent, in signum prsesumptionis gladios suos, [quos] irreverenter contra Sancti Edmundi libertatem erexerant, veniam petentes feretro martyris optulerunt. Istud miraculum sculptum est in choro cum aliis miraculis juxta sedem abbatis, cum his versibus:

Hic rapiuntur equi de fundo martyris aequi;
Clamant raptores, faciunt patiendo dolores;
Post veniunt flentes, enses offere volentes,
Abbatem quaerunt, contritti corde fuerunt;
Hos absolvebat humiles quos esse videbat.

86. De Translatione Veteris Ecclesiae Saresberiensis et Constructione Novae. **R.S.** LVII, III, 189. Event, 1237.
Number of lines not ascertained.

(The complete poem is inaccesible to me; many chronicles quote this couplet):

——— ——— ——— ——— ——— ———   l. 1
Rex igitur det opes, praesul det opem, lapicidae   l. 205.
Dent operum; tribus his est opus, ut stet opus.

87. Dialogue Between Henry de Lacy and Walter Biblesworth on The Crusade. **R.A.**, I, 134.
Event, 1270.   72 ll.
Sire Gautier, dire viis voil

88. On the Length of Henry III's Reign. **A.L.**, 243.
C. 1272.   4 ll.
Septuaginta duo fuerant et mille ducenti,
Quando vir hic obiit, post partum Virginis anni;
Per quinquaginta sex annos atque diebus
Bis decies regnum rexerat iste suum.

89. Satire on the Ladies. **R.A.** I, 162.
Date not given.   62 ll.
Ici commence la jeste des dames.
Quei diroms des dames kaunt vienent a festes,   l. 1

90. Satire on the Blacksmiths. **R.A.**, I, 240.
Date not given.   22 ll.
Swarte smekyd smethes smateryd with smoke

EDWARD I.

A. ENGLAND

91. Song on the Venality of the Judges. C.S. VI, 224.
Date, not certainly known.   144 ll.
   Beati qui esuriunt.
92. A Satyre on the Consistory Courts. C.S. VI, p. 155.
Date, not certainly known.   90 ll.
   Ne mai no lewed lued libben in londe.
93. A Song on the Times. C.S. VI, 195. Date, not certainly known.   198 ll.
   Whose thenchith up this carful lif.
94. Song against the King's Taxes. C.S. VI, 182.
1297+(?)   85 ll.
   Dieu, roy de mageste, ob personas trinas,
95. Song of the Husbandman. C.S. VI, p. 149. 1297 or
later. (T.W.) (?)   72 ll.
   Ich herde men upo mold make muche mon.
96. The Outlaw's Song of Traillebaston. C.S. VI, 231.
Date, not certainly known.   98 ll.
   Talent me prent de rymer e de geste fere.
97. On the Destruction of False Money. R.S. XCV, III,
106. Decreed December 26, 1298.   2 ll.
   Anno MCCXCIX', celebravit rex Nativitatem Domini
Westmonasterii qui videns Angliam plurimum corrumpi
falsa moneta quae crokard et pollard dicebatur, in die sancti
Stephani pro perpetuo deleri prsecepit. Hinc quidam
lathomi filius, opera patris sui considerans, metrice scripsit.
   Laude decoreris noster starlinge gereris,
   Crokar es, aesque peris, fugias as rite teneris.

B. FRANCE.

98. A Poem on the Loss of Gascony. R.S. XII, II, I, 164.
c. 1293, from its place in the Chronicle.   68 ll.
   Satis novit saeculum
   De lingua Gallorum
99. On the Execution of Thomas Turbeville, a Traitor. R.S.
XCV, III, 282. Event, Oct 8, 1295.   8 ll.
   The Flores Historiarum devotes over a page to Turbe-
ville's treason, trial and execution. The account concludes

thus: Bacillis eorum fuscinulisque illusus, sic patibulo est
affixus, ut sepulturam secundum comitum jussa non reciperet
corpus ejus, ita ut praetereuntes dicerent, "Hiccine est
Thomas Turbevile?" Cui quidam versificator epitaphium
scripsit hoc modo:

Turbat tranquilla clam Thomam Turbida villa,
Qui quasi scintilla fuit, accidit ecce favilla.
Cum Sathanae turbis est vici, scopa fit urbis,
Stratus pelle bovis, frustratur Gallica quo vis.
Terram turbavit Thomas, haec hunc cruciavit.
Hinc cum se stravit quem bis, ter, equus laceravit,
Achitophel perit, aspera David modo quaerit,
Thomam pependit, Anglos dum munere vendit.

C. WALES

100.   Rival Elegies on Llywelyn. **R.S.** XLI, VIII, 267. Date
of death, 1282.   4+4=8 ll.
(In many chronicles, sometimes separately.)

And after that, abowte the feste of seynte Lucy, the hedde
of Lewelyne was sende to kynge Edwarde, and after to London.   And David, brother to the said Lewelyn, mover and
causer of that tribulacion, was taken soone after, and was
condempnede at the grete parliamente at Schrobbesbery,
drawen with horses firste, and hongede afterwarde, and after
that his body divided into iiij. partes, and sende to diverse
places of Ynglonde.   Too religious men, oon of Ynglonde,
an other of Wales, made versus of the seide Lewelyn, prynce
of Wales.   The religious man of Wales did wryte of hym in
this wyse:

[a.] "Hic jacet Anglorum tortor, tutor Venedorum,
Princeps Wallorum Lewelihus, regula morum,
Gemma coevorum, flos regum preteritorum,
Forma futurorum; dux, laus, lex, lux populorum."

The Ynglische man did wryte in this wyse:

[b.] "Hic jacet errorum princeps et predo virorum,
Proditor Anglorum, fax livida, secta reoram,
Numen Wallorum, trux dux, homicida piorum,
Fex Trojanorum, stirps mendax, causa malorum."

D. SCOTLAND.

101.   A Jeer at the Scots. C.S. VI, 391. Date uncertain. 3 11
Tprut! Skot riveling,
In unseli timing

crope thu out of cage.

102. Scotch Rime on Edw. I.   T. W's L.&S. 261.
c. 1296, as it refers to the siege of Berwick.   5 ll.
What wenys king Edward with his long shankes
To have wonne Berwike, all our unthankes.
Gaas pykes hym,
And when he hath it
Gaas dykes hym.

103. Scotch Satire adapted after the Taking of Berwick.
T. W. ed. R.S. XLVII, II, 234. c. 1296.   18 ll.
Pierre de Langtoft describes the taking of Berwick in
some detail. His account of the siege concludes thus:
Li rays Eduuard la teent conquis par espe,
[Le fet environer de fosse large e lee.]
En reprovaunt le Escot, ke ad de ly chaunte,
Et par mokerye en Euglays rymeye:
Pykit him,
An diket hym,
On scoren sayd he;
He dikes, he pikes,
On lenche als hym likes,
Hu best may be.

104. Song of Balliol's Men before Dunbar. T. W. ed. R.S.
XLVII, II, 244. Event, 1296.   18 ll.
De nos enemys,
Kant scrount pris,
Mercy nul en ait.

105. Song in Mockery of the Scots after Dunbar. T. W. ed.
R.S. XLVII, II. 248. c. 1296.   12 ll.
The fote folk
Put the Scottes in the polk
And nackened thair nages.

106. Rejoicing over Scots after Dunbar. T.W. ed. R.S.
XLVII, II, 252. c. 1296.   6 ll.
For Scottes,
Telle i for sottes,
And wrecches unwar;
Unsele
Dintes to dele
Tham drohu to Dumbar.

107. Exhortation to Edw. I to do strict Justice on the Scotch
Prisoners. T. W. ed. R.S. XLVII, II, 254. c. 1296.   54 ll.
Calays, Yrays,
A nos Englays

Aident durement;
108.   Satirical Verses on the Scotch after Edw.'s First Conquest. T. W. ed. **R.S.** XLVII, II, 260. Event, 1296.   42 ll.
Les XII peres
S'e(n)vount a freres,
Pur els confesser;
109.   On Edward's Victories thruout the British Isles.
T. W. ed. **R.S.** XLVII, II, 266 c. 1296, from its connection
with the preceding.   36 ll.
Ses enemys,
Deus Mercys!
Sunt chastiez;
110.   Ten Latin Prophecies to terrify the Scots. T. W. ed.
R. S. XLVII, II, 448. Dates uncertain.   85 ll.
(These poems, like those on the death of Richard I, occur
elsewhere separately. Cf. j with No. 115).
    a.   Regnum Scotorum fuit inter caetera regna   (12 ll.)
    b.   Principe magnifico tellus viduata vacabit
        Annis bis trinis mensibus atque novem.   (2 ll.)
    c.   Antiquos reges, justos, largos, locupletes,   (5 ll.)
    d.   Pro dolor! Albania fraude subacta sua.   (1 l.)
    e.   Quod respirabit post funus regis avari.   (1 l.)
    f.   Cum fuerint anni completi mille ducenti   (7 ll.)
    g.   Rex borialis erit numerosa classe potitus,
        Affligens Scotos ense, furore, fame.   (2 ll.)
    h.   Extra gens tandem Scotorum fraude peribit,
        In bello princeps notus ipse vel ense cadet,
        Gallicia quem genuit, qui gazis regna replebit,
        Proh dolor! o gemitus! fratris ab ense cadet. (4 ll.)
    i.   Candidus Albanus, patriotis causa ruinae,   (21 ll.)
    j.   (Versus de Prophetiis Merlini.)
        Ecce dies veniunt, Scoti sine principe fiunt, (30 ll.)
111.   Allegorical Prophecy on the Scotch Wars. T. W. ed.
R.S. XLVII, II, 452. Date uncertain.   128 ll.
Als y yod on ay Mounday bytwene Wyltinden and Walle,
112.   Fragment on the Capture of Dunbar. T. W. ed. **R.S.**
XLVII, II, x. Date uncertain.   9 ll.
For thar wer thai brend,
He kauged ham thidre kend,
Ant dreved to dote.
113.   On the Welsh at Falkirk. **R.S.** CXIV, 187. Event,
July 22, 1298.   2 ll.
Rex Edwarde, fidem si des Wallensibus, erras,
Ut dederas pridem; sed eorum diripe terras.

114. Song on the Scottish Wars. C.S. VI, 160. After
Falkirk, 1298.   268 ll.
 Ludere volentibus ludens paro lyram;
115. On the Deposition of Balliol. C.S. VI, 180. After
Balliol's retreat to Normandy, 1299.   30 ll.
(Same as No. 110j.)
 Ecce dies venient Scoti sine principe fiunt;
116. The Roll of Caerlaverock. R. of C. ed. T. W.
Event, 1300.   958 ll.
(The arms of the nobles assembled by Edw. I. to invade Scot-
land.)
 En cronicles de granz moustiers
117. On the Murder of John Comyn by Robert Bruce. R.S.
XCV, III, 323. Event, February 10, 1305.   3 ll.
 Ecclesiae navis titubat, regni quia clavis
 Errat; rex, Papa, facti sunt unica capa;
 Haec faciunt do des, Pilatus hic, alter Herodes.
118. On the Execution of William Wallace. T. W. ed. R.S.
XLVII, II, 364. Event, Aug. 23, 1305.   12 ll.
 Pierre de Langtoft gives some details of Wallace's cap-
ture and execution. His account ends:
 Cope li fust le cors en quatre porciouns;
 Chescun pende par say, en memor de ses nouns,
 En lu de sa banere cels sunt ces gunfanouns.
   Pur finer sa geste
   A Loundres est sa teste,
     Du cors est fet partye
   En iiij. boncs vilcs,
   Dount honurer les ylles
     Ke sunt en Albanye.
   And tus may you here
   A ladde to lere
     To bigken in pais;
   It falles in his eghe
   That hackes ovre heghe,
     Wit at Walays.
119. Song on the Execution of Sir Simon Fraser. C.S. VI,
212. Nov. 7, 1306.   272 ll.
 Lystneth, lordynges, a newe song ichulle bigynne,
120. On the Conquest of Scotland. R.S. CXIV, 408.
Date uncertain.   12 ll.
 The Annales Angliae et Scotiae concludes with the year
1300, just as Edward I, enraged at the loss of Stirling, vowed
to be revenged on the Scots. Illo eodem tempore, Dominus

Rex legatos, cum epistolis, misit Romae.

Explicit Epistola directa Domino Papae por Regem Angliae. De ista materia Chronigraphus, metrice scribens, breviter sic ait.

Edwardus Rex Anglus Scotos expugnavit,
Eorum hostiliter vires enervavit,
Walliam que Scotiam sibi subjugavit.
Willelmus Wales, dux Scotorum, latitavit.
Tandem captus vinclis strictis mancipatur,
Et ductus Londonias, ibi judicatur;
Tractus que suspensus est, tandem decollatur:
Qui primo risit, post haec merito lecrymatur.
Talis in memoria Rex sit sempiterna,
Qui rebelles subditos compulit aeterna
Sua mala plangere, novaque moderna;
In collis anima requiescat pace superna.

E. ELEGIAC POEMS.

121. Elegy on Walter de Merten, Bishop of Rochester. **R.S.** XXXVI, IV, 275. Date of death, Oct. 27, 1277.   10 ll.

The Annales de Oseneia, under 1277, says: Eodem anno in vigilia Apostolorum Simonis et Judae [Oct. 27] obiit dominus Walterus de Mertone, episcopus Roffensis, de cujus moribus quidam versificator dixit:

"Praesul Walterus Roffensis pontificali
Culmine sincerus, virtute micans speciali,
Qui de Mertona vulgari more vocatus,
Cujus fama bona, gestus super omnia gratus,
Fidus in alloquio, justus, sermone modestus,
Cautus consilio, castus, socialis, honestus,
Dilexit clerum, gratis tribuens alimentum,
Pro quo Walterum benedicit turma studentum;
Oxoniae studium per eum quasi plantula vernat.
Conferat auxilium sibi Rex qui cuncta gubernat."

122. On the Death of Prince Alfonso. **R.S.** CXIV., 481. Date of death, 1258.   5 ll.

Alfundi vitam planget gens tota sopitam;
Anglicus, Hispanus, flos qui fuit, est modo vanus.
Spes populi, regnique decus, clerique levamen,
De medio rapuit, heu! miseranda caedes.
Flos juvenum, spes militum, patrisque solamen.

123. Verses on Tomb of Edward I. **F.** 405. Date of death, 1307.   24 ll.

Mors est mesta nimis, magnos quia iugit in imis.

124. Elegiac Couplet on Edward I. R.S. XCII, 10. (Quot.
from Fabyan.) Date of death, 1307.   2 ll.
Dum viuit rex, et valuit sua magna potestas,
Fras, latuit, pax magna fuit, regnauit honestas.
125. Lament on the Death of Edward I. C.S. VI, 241.
Date of death, 1307.   82 ll.
Seigniurs, orez, pur Dieu le grant,
126. Elegy on the Death of Edward I. C.S. VI, 246. Date
of death, July 7, 1307.   91 ll.
Alle that beoth of huerte trewe,

F. ON THE CONTINENT (excluding France)
127. Song on the Flemish Insurrection. C.S. VI, 187.
c. 1302-7. (T.W.)   136 ll.
Lustneth, lordinges, bothe yonge ant olde,
Of the Freynsshe-men that were so proude ant bolde,

G. POEMS ON MISCELLANEOUS SUBJECTS
128. The Praise of the Young Edward. C.S. VI, 128.
c. 1272. (T.W.)   82 ll.
Eaduuardi regis Anglorum me pepulere
129. A Song of the Times. C.S. VI, 133. "Soon after his
accession." (T.W.) (?)   32 ll.
Vulneratur karitas, amor aegrotatur; (or)
Amur gist en maladie, charite est nafri,
130. Political Scraps, on the Degeneracy of the Present
Time. R.A. II, 121. Date uncertain.   4+4=8 ll.
a. Men hem bimenis of litel trewthe,
It is ded and that is rewthe;
Lesing livet and is above,
And now is biried trewthe and love!
b. Now goot falshed in evri flok,
And trewthe is sperd under a lok:
Now no man may comen therto,
But yef he singge si dedero.
131. To John de Kirkeby. Chancellor (and Bp. of Ely)
R.S. XVI, 167. Date not ascertained.   6 ll.
Non est inventus similis tibi Kirkebyensis,
132. On a Franciscan, killed for betraying a Confession.
R.S. XXXVI, IV, 513. Event, 1293.   2 ll.
Mos hujus terrae non est confessa referre;
Funus Walteri super hoc vult testis haberi,
qui existens lector fratrum Minorum Herefordiae, cujus-
dam viri confessionem audivit et eam detexit. Unde postea
confitens erubuit, et in ira fratrem illum cum secure in capite

percussit, et ei imposuit silentium sempiternum.

133. A Song against the Retinues of the Great People. C.S.
VI, 237. 1300-1325. (T.W.) (?)   80 ll.
       Of ribaudz y ryme
134. Against the Pride of the Ladies. C.S. IV, 153.
1250-1300.   35 ll.
       Lord that lenest us lyf, ant lokest uch an lede,
135. On the Great Wind of 1299. R.S. XXXVI, IV, 543.
Event, 1299.   5 ll.
       Ventus ut insanus perflavit meridianus
       Quercus prostravit, aedes magnas violavit,
       Radices flamen confregerat ut leve stramen,
       Sunt exstirpata vento pomeria lata,
       Ferro firmata sunt campanaria strata.
136. Song against the Scholastic Studies. C.S. VI, 206.
Date uncertain.   84 ll.
       Meum est propositum gentis imperitae
137. The Song of Nego. C.S. VI, 210. Date uncertain. 24 ll.
       Hit nis bot trewth, I wend, an afte
138. Sir Pride the Emperor..R.A. II, 248. —early in the
XIV century (W. & H.) (?)   311 ll.
       Sire Orguylle ly emperour
       Enveyt ses lettris par cy entour,
         Escotez, seyngnours, un tretiz   l. 1
       De moun sir Orguyl ly positifs,

H. IRELAND.

139. On a Riot between Irish and English Friars at Cork.
R.S. XXXVI, IV, 506. c. 1291, by its place in the Chronicle.
                                                        2 ll.
       Quarto idus Junii in Hybernia apud Corc, fratrum
Minorum fuit capitulum generale; ubi fratres Hybernenses
venerunt armati cum quadam bulla; pro qua orta conten-
tione contra Anglicos pugnaverunt, et multis mortuis et vul-
neratis hinc inde, Anglici tandem urbis auxilio cum
ordinis scandalo superabant.
       Bullae papales sunt fratribus exitiales;
       Qui quondam mites, faciunt nunc praelia, lites.
140. A Satire on the People of Kildare. ("Of Men Lif That
Wonith in Lond.") R.A. II, 174, c. 1300. (T. W.)   120 ll.
       Hail seint Michael with e lange sper!
141. A Song in Praise of Sir Piers de Birmingham. R. A. S.
and B. I, 70. Date of death, 1308.   132 ll.
       Sith Gabriel gan grete

EDWARD II.

A. EDWARD VS. THE BARONS

142. On the King's Breaking his Confirmation of Magna
Charta.   C.S. VI, 253.   c. 1311.   98 ll.

L'en puet fere et defere,
    Ceo fiat-il trop sovent;
It nis nouther wel ne faire;
    Therfore Engelond is shent.

143. Songs on the Death of Peter de Gaveston.   C.S. VI,
258. Date of death, June 19, 1312.   28+30=58 ll.
    a.   Vexilla regni proderunt,
    b.   Pange, lingua, necem Petri qui turbavit Angliam.

144. On Edw. II's Oppression of the Church.   R.S. CXV,
142.   c. 1323.   4 ll.

The St. Alban's Henrici de Blaneforde Chronica gives
an extended account of the confiscation of the property
of the Bishop of Hereford.   It then notes, in a sentence, the
restoration of the possessions of the Bishop of Lincoln, for
over two years held by the king.   The chronicle continues:
Quidam insuper, cautela injecta excellenter instructus,
videns confusionem cleri et perturbationem non modicam
praelatorum, hos veridicos versus protulit, in haec verba;

"Nostri cornuti sunt consilio quasi muti
    Et quia non tuti, nequeunt sermonibus uti.   Versus
Sunt quasi confusi decreto legis abusi.   optimi.
Sic perit Ecclesia, juris et ipsa via."

145. In Mockery of Hugh Despenser, Jr., at his Execution.
R.S. CXVI, I, 185.   Event, 1326.   2 ll.

As Hugh Despenser was led on horseback thru the
streets of Hereford to his execution he wore a vestment
bearing the following mocking poem, in addition to the first
seven verses of the LVII psalm ("Why boastest thou thy-
self—")

Funus cum lignis, ate miser ensis et ignis,
    Hugo securis, equus, abstulit omne decus.

146. A "Prophecy" on the Despensers.   R.S. LXXVI, II,
89.   c. 1326, by its place in the Chronicle.   6 ll.

The Gesta Edwardi de Carnarvan Auctore Bridlingtoniensi quotes in full the sentence on the younger Despenser
and then concludes the matter thus: unde versus vaticinii;

No.

"Dispensatores hircus vehet hic ad honores,
Qui sibi majores non tractabunt per amores.
Pro fastu natus periet pater inveteratus;
Amorum flores veteres perdentque labores,
Abscisis capita raro remeat quia vita,
Membratim cesus dici poterit male Iesus."

147. "Prophetic" Verses on Edward II. R.S. LXXVI, II,
92. Date uncertain.   18 ll.
Transmittent Britones hircum sed non rationes.

B. SCOTLAND.

148. The Battle of Bannockburn. C.S. VI, 262. c. 1314.
                                                       112 ll.
Me cordis augustia cogit mira fari.

149. A Scotch Taunt after Bannockburn. R. S.S. p. xxvi.
Event, 1314.   6 ll.
Maydens of Englande, sore may ye morne,
For your lemmans ye have lost at Bannockysborne,
   With heue a lowe.
What! weneth the king of England
So soone to have wone Scotlande?
   Myth rumbylowe.

Ritson quotes Fabyan: "Thys songe," he adds, "was after many daies song in daunces in the carols of the maidens and mynstrelles of Scotland, to the reprofe and disdayne of Englyshemen, with dyuers other, whych," says he, "I ouerpasse."

C. ELEGIAC POEMS

150. Epitaph on John Duns Scotus. C.H. I, 234. Date of death, 1308.   4 ll.
Duns Scotus died in 1308, at Cologne, where his tomb in the Franciscan Church bears the inscription:
   Scotia me genuit.
   Anglia me suscepit
   Gallia me docuit.
   Colonia me tenet.

151. On the death of Edw. II. R.S. LXXVI, II, 97. Date of death, 1327.   6 ll.
"O qui scripta legis, memor esse velis rogo fati
   Edwardi regis de Carnervan vocitati;
In cujus gestis Anglis, Kambris, manifestis
   Armatis maestis occurrit plurima pestis;

Edwardum regem Gloucestria condit humatum,
Ad propriumque gregem ducas, bone Christe, beatum.''

D. POEMS ON MISCELLANEOUS SUBJECTS

152. Adam Davy's Five Dreams about Edw. II. **E.E.T.S.**,
C.S. LXIX, ii. Date uncertain.   166 ll.
To our lorde Jesu crist in hevene,
153   On the Seizure of the Templars. **R.S.** LXXVI, II, 32.
Event, Jan. 12, 1308.   1 l.
The Gesta Edwardi de Carnarvan Auctore Bridlingtoni-
ensi deals in detail with the proceedings against the Templars.
The account of their imprisonment concludes: quorum bona
et praedia confiscantur, tantummodo singulis dictorum.
Templariorum ad sustentationem iiii ᵒʳ denariis diebus singulis liberatis, prout metrice dicitur;
''Templis exilium dat ovis et lilium;''
Et postea mittebantur diversis domibus religiosorum possess-
ionatorum commorandos decretum consilii expectantes.
154. On the Birth of Edw. III. **R.S.** LXXVI, II, 45.
Event, Nov. 13, 1312.   4 ll.
Item eodem anno circa mediam horam noctis praeceden-
tis festum Sancti Bricii episcopi et confessoris, natus est Ed-
wardus tertius post conquaestum et sextus post Brutum;
unde scribitur versus:—
Hunc natum cura, virgo vincens nocitura,
Casta creatura, quae salvasti peritura,
De puero pura specialis sit tibi cura,
Ut permansura sibi semper sint sua jura.
155. On the Corruption of Juries. **R.S.** LXXVI, II, 213.
c. 1315.   4 ll.
Under the year 1315 the Vita Edwardi Secundi Auctore
Malmesberiensi devotes a paragraph to the deaths of the earls
of Gloucester and of Warwick. The author takes this as a
judgment of God because of England's sins and devotes his
next paragraph to the great natural faults of the English:
pride, craft and perjury. A third paragraph runs: Omnes
fere lites et placita quae agitantur in regis curia per assisas
terminantur in patria. Porro cum ad assisam ventum fuerit,
qui plus dare sufficit proculdubio optinebit. Heu omnis
religio,omnis dignitas, et omnis potestas cedit pretio. Hinc
quidam festive ait,
Manus ferens munera pium facit impium;
Nummus jungit foedera, dat nummus consilium.

Nummus in praelatis est pro jure satis,
Vos qui judicatis nummo locum datis.

The succeeding paragraph continues the account of the signs of God's displeasure—floods, destruction of hay, and the loss of sheep and other stock.

156. Song on the Times. C.S. VI, 251. "earlier years of Edw.'s reign.'' (T.W.)   36 ll.

Quant honme deit parleir, videat quae verba loquatur;
Sen covent aver, ne stultior inveniatur.
Quando quis loquitur, bote resoun reste therynne,

157. A Poem on the Times of Edw. II, **P.S.** XXVII. 1313-1320. (?)   858 ll.

Why werre and wrake in londe

158. The Lady and her Dogs. **R.A.** I, 155. Date uncertain.   68 ll.

Veez cy solaz de une dame,
Courteyse e de bone fame.
Jeo say un dame de bone purveaunce, l. 1,
Si vous assentez a son ordenaunce,

EDWARD III.

A. THE FRENCH WAR.

159. On Edward's Invasion of France. **R.S**. XCIII, 83.
Event, 1338. 4 ll.
 M simplex, c. ter, x. triplex, v. semel, i ter,
 Belliger E. ter rex trans mare sumpsit iter;
 Ortus vigeno sexto, regni duodeno,
 X. V. lux Julii fit sibi navigii.
160. The Vows of the Heron. P. P. & S., I. 1.
Event, 1338. 440 ll.
 Ens cl mois de Setembre, qu'estes va a dedin,
161. Edward's Invasion of Brabant. P. P. & S., I, 63.
Event, 1338. 126 ll.
 How Edward the king come in Braband,
162. Philip's Flight from before Edward. P. P. & S., I, 66.
Event, 1338. 96 ll.
 Edward oure cumly king,
163. Epigram on the Assumption of the Arms of France.
P. P. & S., I, 26. Event, 1339. 5 ll.
 Rex sum regnorum bina ratione duorum;
164. The Battle in the Swyn. P. P. & S., I, 70. 1340. 88 ll.
 Minot with mowth had menid to make
165. The Siege of Tournay. P. P. & S., I, 72, 1340. 81 ll.
 Tourenay, yow has tight
166. An Invective against France. P. P. & S., I, 26.
1346. 391 ll.
 Francia, foeminea, pharisaea, vigoris idea,
167. Edward's Landing at Hogges and Invasion of France.
P. P. & S., I, 75. 1346. 172 ll.
 Men may rede in Romance right (or)
 A Bore es broght on bankes bare,
168. The Siege of Calais. P. P. & S., I, 80. 1347. 96 ll.
 Calais men, now may ye care,
169. On the Truce of 1347. P. P. & S., I, 53. 1347. 149 ll.
 Cantica laetitiae mundi flos Anglia promat,
170. The Capture of Gynes. P. P. & S., I, 89. 1352. 80 ll.
 War this winter oway,
171. On Robert Knollys at Poitiers. **R.S**. XXXVI, III, 476.
Event, 1356. 2 ll.

In the Annales de Bermundesia a very brief notice of the battle of Poitiers concludes thus: In isto bello de Roberto Knollis milite Cestriae sic canebatur metrice:

O Robert Knollis, per te fit Francia mollis;
Ense tuo tollis praedas, dans vulnera collis.

172.　The Dispute between the Englishman and the Frenchman. P. P. & S., I, 91.　　　　　　　　　　　　　72 ll.

Anglia, faex hominum, pudor orbis, et ultima rerum.

173.　The "Prophecies" of John of Bridlington. P. P. & S., I, 123. c. 1370. (?) (The numerous versions of some of the "prophecies" make the determination of the date of writing more complex than Wright indicates. See No. 192.)　660 ll.

Febribus infectus, requies fuerat mihi lectus,

B.　ENGLISH AFFAIRS

(Here again, as in the lack of political poems referring to the signing of Magna Charta, the absence of allusions in verse to a particular subject is worthy of notice. The importance of the growth of parliamentary power under Edward III and the change in the habits of the people marked by the introduction of English as the language of the law courts instead of French are well-nigh as common-place as John's struggle with the Barons. The French war and the black death are, respectively, in close causal relation to the rise of parliamentary power and the celebrated Statute of Laborers of 1351. (Mackinnon) The war and the plague figure in the political verse of the time but the two latter are not mentioned, nor are such prominent features of the reign as the Statutes of Provisors and Praemunire and the Good Parliament.)

C.　SCOTCH WARS.

174.　A Scotch Rime ridiculing English Costume. **L. & S.** 260-261.　c. 1329.　(T.W.)　　　　　　　　　　　　4 ll.

Long beerdis hartles
Poynted　hoodes coytles
Gay cottes gracelis
Maketh Englande thryfteles.

175.　Ercyldoun's Prophecy. **R.A.** I, 30.
Date uncertain.　　　　　　　　　　　　　　　　　10 ll.

To nyght is boren a barn in Kaernervam,
That ssal wold the out ydlis ylc an.
The kyng Alesandre acsede,

Hwan sall that be? The menstral zede;
Hwan Banockesbourne is y-det myd mannis bonis;
Hwan hares kendleth in hertth-stanes;
Hwan laddes weddeth levedes;
Hwan me ledeth men to selle wyth rapis;
Hwan Rokysburth is no burth;
Hwan men gyven an folu of twenti pound for an seme
    of hwete.
176. Prophecies Relating to Edward III. **R.A.**II, 25,
(cf. 245). Date uncertain.   75 ll.
Versus inventi Londoni in una pila de corio, de Rege
Edwardo iii' post conquestum.
    En pila regalis vocitor, tum ludus ejusdem. l. l.
    Versus vaticanales editi a Gilda hystoriographo.
    Regnum Scotorum fuit inter caetera regna   l. 38.
177. Verses on the Defeat of the Boastful Scots Under
Edward Baliol. **R.S.** LXXVI, II, 102-3. c. 1332.   23 ll.
    Rem referam gestam, multis populis manifestam,
178. The Battle of Halidon Hill. P. P. & S., I, 58.
Event, 1333.   94 ll.
    Trew king, that sittes in trone,
179. Edward's Vengeance for Bannockburn. P. P. & S.,
I, 61. c. 1333.   38 ll.
    Skottes out of Berwik and of Abirdene,
180. I. On the Battle of Nevile's Cross. P. P. & S., I, 40.
Event, Oct. 17, 1346.   26 ll.
    Si valeas paleas, Valoyes, dimitte timorem;
181. II. On the Battle of Nevile's Cross. P. P. & S., I, 41.
                                                   271 ll.
    Dux Valeys hinnit, Francia grunnit, territa tinnit;
182. On Crecy and Nevile's Cross. P. P. & S., I, 52. Events,
Aug. 26 and Oct. 17, 1346.   31 ll.
    Annis bis sex c., quater x., bis ter, simul et c.,
183. On the Battle of Nevile's Cross. P. P. & S., I, 83.
Event, Oct. 17, 1346.   134 ll.
    Sir David the Bruse
184. A Taunt at the Scots. P. P. & S., I, 52.
Date uncertain.   3 ll.
    Est omnis Scotus Sampson, Salomon, leo totus.
    Sampson se necuit, Salomon post tdola travit,
    Est leo famelicus, sic omnis Scotus iniquus.

D. SPANISH WARS.

185. Edward's Naval Victory. P. P. & S., I, 87.
Event, 1350.   60 ll.
I wald noght spare for to speke,
186. On Prince Edward's Expedition Into Spain. P. P. & S.,
I, 94. Event, 1367.   80 ll.
Gloria cunctorum detur domino dominorum,
187. On Prince Edward's Expedition into Spain and the
Battle of Najara. P. P. & S., I, 97. Event, 1367.   668 ll.
Mi Martonensis, pater amplexandc, Johannes,

E. ELEGIAC POEMS

188. On Adam Orleton, Bishop of Winchester. **R.S.** XCIII,
173. Date of death, 1345.   3 ll.
Item, hoc anno, xviij. die mensis Julii, obiit dominus
Adam de Orletone, Wyntoniensis episcopus, senex et plenus
dierum, postquam ecclesias Herefordiensem, Wygorniensem,
et Wyntoniensem ambitiosque quaesitas, viginti octo annis,
duobus mensibus et amplius rexerat successive. Note 1: At
the foot of the page in H the following verses are written
in a later hand:
Trigamus est Adam, ductus cupidine quadam.
Thomam neglexit; Wolstanum non bene rexit;
Swithunum maluit. Cur? Quia plus valuit.
189. On John de Vere. VII Earl of Oxford. **A.L.**(C.S.
XXXIV), ccxxi, n. Date of death, 1360.   4 ll.
Stapleton's preface, note to p. ccxxi. . . . . . The famil-
ies of Beaumont and Vere were nearly related through the
marriage of Henry, fifth Lord Beaumont with Margaret,
daughter of John de Vere, seventh Earl of Oxford. In the
east window of the church of Barton-upon-Humber is still
remaining a portraiture of this nobleman in painted glass;
and beneath was this tetrastick: ,
Rex Hierosolymus cum Bellomonte locatur,
Bellusmons iterum cum Boghan consociatur;
Bellusmons iterum cum Longicastro religatur,
Bellusmons [sponsalibus] Oxonie titulatur.
The word between brackets wanting in the original, thus
supplied by Mr. Segar, was doubtless a third repetition of the
word "iterum."
190. I. On the Death of Edward III. P. P. & S., I, 215.
Date of death, 1377.   112 ll.
A! dere God, what may this be,

191. II. On the Death of Edward III. Date of death, 1377.
P. P. & S., I, 219.   179 ll.
Regis in Edwardi bene debeo funere flere,

F. POEMS ON MISCELLANEOUS SUBJECTS.

192. How Edward III obtained the Crown. **R.S.** LXXVI,
II, 97-98. Event, 1327.   8 ll.
After a poem on the death of Edward II, (No. 151), the
Gesta Edwardi Tertii Auctore Bridlingtoniensi goes on: De
regis hujus decessu varia vulgariter opinantur, de qua materia
ulterius disserere jam non curo, quia scribitur versus:—
 Credo quod interdum multis mendacia prosunt,
 Et quandoque nocet omnia vera loqui,
 Vera loqui nocuit, nocuit nimis esse fidelem,
 Res ea me docuit ne cunctis cuncta revelem.
 Exiet et rediet firmatus nomine patris
 Ejus et interiet genitor terebratus in atris.
 Arte suae matris regnum rapiet sibi patris
 Funera post patris quaeret regalia matris.
 Sed quod in vaticinio metrico de domino rege nostro nunc
et patre suo dicitur audiamus versus.
 Ll. 5-8, as well as a nine line "prophecy" on page 96 are
from the Prophecy of John of Bridlington (No. 173), one of
the most widely circulated of this class of works.
193. A Prophecy foretelling the rule of Edward III. **R.S.**
LXXVI, II, 93. Event, 1327.   2 ll.
 The Gesta Edwardi de Carnarvan Auctore Bridlingtoni-
ensi gives a detailed and interesting account of how the following prophecy of Edward III's accession was revealed to
St. Thomas, Archbishop of Canterbury at a time when there
was discord between Henry II and Henry, his eldest son and
crowned heir. This the author considers a good omen for
Edward III's reign.
 H. patre submarcet post R. reget J. que relicto
 E. post H. rex fit, E. post E. postea mira.
194. On the Tournament. **R.S.** LXXVI, I, 355. Event,
Sept. 23-25, 1331.   2 ll.
 Anno Dei xi° cubice nonoque kalendas
 Tobis trina dies hastas Edwarde Chep en das.
195. On the Discouragements to Literary Distinction. **R.S.**
LXVI, II, 25, 1339 (?) (May be older than context.) 54 ll.
 Scriberem dictanda varia
196. On the Plague in 1348-9. **R.S.** XXXVI, III, 475. 1 l.

The Annales de Bermundesia has the following account of the black plague: Anno Domini MCCCXLVIII., et anno regni regis Edwardi tertii vicesimo tertio. Hoc anno incepit magna pestilentia Londonise, circa festum Sancti Michaelis, et duravit usque ad festum Sancti Petri ad Vincula proximo sequens. Ista pestilentia vix reliquit decimum hominem in Anglia. Unde versus:

Grande fuit funus, ML. ter C. vacat unus.

197. I. On the Great Wind in 1361-2. **R.S.** I, 221.   2 ll.

C. ter erant mille decies [sex] unus et ille
Luce tua Maure vehemens fuit impetus aure.
A thousand III. hundred sexti and too,
Was Maurus wynd whech blew soo.

198. II. On the Great Wind in 1361-2. **R.S.** XXXVI, III, 477.   1 l.

Ecce flat hoc anno Maurus, in orbe tonat.

199. On the Black Prince's Quarrel with Hampden. **H-P.** P.R. and N.T. p. 194. Date uncertain.   3 ll.

Hamden of Hamden did forgoe
The manors of Tring, Wing and Ivinghoe,
For striking the Black Prince a blow.

200. Verses on the Conqueror's Founding Battle Abbey. **R.A.** I, 92. c. 1366. (?) (Date uncertain; likely slightly earlier, if the "prophecy" was written for political effect.) 8 ll.

Anglorum regna Bastard bello superavit,
Ac monasterium rex construere properavit;
Jejuans, orans, volens de sobole scire,
Divum responsum rex promeretur audire:
'Quot pedibus stabit ecclesia Battalia longa,
Tot annis tua posteritas stabit in Angla,'
Quam licet ecclesiam prolongasse voluere,
Trecentos pedos excedere non potuere.

RICHARD II.

A. *THE PEASANT REVOLT.*

201. First Epistle of John Ball. **P.S.** I, sec. 7, p. 2.
c. 1381.   8 ll.
    John the Miller hath yground small, small,
202. Second Epistle of John Ball. **P.S.** I, sec. 7, p. 2.
c. 1381.   13 ll.
    John Ball, St. Mary priest,
203. Jack Miller's Song. **P.S.** I, sec. 7, p. 3. c. 1381. 17 ll.
    Jack Miller asketh helpe to turn his Mill aright.
204. Jack Trueman's Epistle. **P.S.** I, sec. 7, p. 4.
c. 1381.   11 ll.
    Jack Trewman doeth you to understond
205. On the Rebellion of Jack Straw. P. P. & S., I, 224.
c. 1381. (See No. 215).   74 ll.
    Tax has tenet us alle,
        probat hoc mors tot validorum,
    The kyng thereof hade smalle,
        fuit in manibus cupidorum,
206. On the Slaughter of Archbishop Sudbury. P. P. & S.,
I, 227. Event, 1381.   108 ll.
    Proh dolor! accrevit nuper confusio rerum;

B. *LOLLARDRY.*

207. Against the Lollards. P. P. & S., I, 231. c. 1381. 672 ll.
    Praesta, Jhesu, quod postulo,
208. On the Council of London. P. P. & S., I, 253. Event,
May 19, 1382.   294 ll.
    Heu! quanta desolatio Angliae praestatur,
    Cujus regnum quodlibet hinc inde minatur,
    Et hujus navigium pene conquassatur;
    Regnum nec consilio nec ope juvatur.
        With an O and an I, prae dolore ventris,
        Meum jam consilium jacet in vi mentis.
209. On the Lollards burning an Image of St. Katherine.
R.S. XCII, II, 183. Event, 1382.   28 ll.
    Olim quippe viri fuerant duo valde nefandi,
210. Verses posted by the Lollards on the Door of St. Paul's.
R.S. CXV, 182 .Event, 1395.   6 ll.

Hii versus qui sequuntur, affixi fuere ostio Sancti
Pauli;—
"Plangant Anglorum gentes crimen sodomorum;
Paulus fert, horum sunt idola causa malorum.
Surgunt ingrati Giazitae, Simone nati,
Nomine praelati, hoc defensare parati.
Qui reges estis, populis quicunque prae estis,
Qualiter hiis gestis gladiis prohibeer potestis?''

C. SPAIN.

(Under Edward III three poems (Nos. 185-187), by
English writers are included which celebrate English victories over the Spanish in that reign. It is highly probable that
an examination of Spanish literature would reveal corresponding Spanish exultations over the numerous unsuccessful ef-
forts of John of Gaunt to make good his title of "King of
Castile.'')

D. IRELAND.

(Richard II's two expeditions into Ireland are probably
reflected in some contemporary political verse. As in Wales,
during Henry III's reign, the death of a chieftain was often
lamented by the bards who recounted the exploits of the de-
parted hero. There are likely many such poems, unpublished
or in rare volumes, on the chiefs who fought Richard so suc-
cessfully during his second expedition of 1399.)

E. ENGLAND.

211. I, On the Earthquake of 1382. P.P.&S., I, 250.
Event, 1382.   88 ll.
     Yit is God a courteis lord,
212. Distich on the Year 1391. P. P. & S., I, 278. Date
uncertain.   2 ll.
     The ax was sharp, the stokke was harde,
     In the xiiij yere of kyng Richarde.
213. On the Pestilence. P. P. & S., I, 279.
Event, 1391 (?)   64 ll.
     Ecce dolet Anglia luctibus imbuta.
214. The Reconciliation of Richard II with the City of
London. P. P. & S., I, 282. Event, August, 1393.   544 ll.
     Tullius in laudem tantam sustollit amicos.
215. On the Arrest of the Duke of Gloucester. **R.S.** CXV,
206. Event, 1397. Prophecy from c. 1387?   2 ll.

After a long and detailed account of the surrender of the Earl of Arundel and the arrest of the Earl of Warwick and the Duke of Gloucester, the Annales Ricardi Secundi, Regis Angliae proceeds: Impletaque fuit tunc prophetia comminatoria, metrice composita, [et] per decennium ante vulgata; quae talis est:—

"Vulpes cum cauda caveat, dum cantat alauda,
Ne rapiens pecus simul rapiatur, et equus."

"Vulpem cum cauda" vocavit Ducem, quia semper ferebatur super hostam, in ejus praesentia, cauda vulpis. "Dum cantat alauda" dixit, quia mane ad cantus alaudae, prout contigit, capiendus fuit; quo capto, imminebat et raptus pecudis repientis, id est, Comitis Warwici; et equi, id est, Comitis Arundeliae; quia alter pro signo ferebat ursum, alter equum.

Cf. T.W.'s version, P.P.& S., 1, 226, (part of No. 205?)

Vulpes cum cauda caneat, cum cantat alauda,
Ne rapide pecus voculus capiatur et equus.

216. On King Richard II.   P.P.&S., I, 360.   Date uncertain.   104 ll.

O Deus immense, sub quo dominantur in ense

217. On the Expected Arrival of the Duke of Lancaster. P. P. & S., I, 366.   Event, July, 1399.   42 ll.

O Deus in collis disponens cuncta fidelis,

218. On King Richard's Ministers.   P.P.&S., I, 363. 1399.   90 ll.

Ther is a busch that is forgrowe;

219. On the Fallen Ministers. **R.S.** CXV, 276, n. 5. c. 1399.   21 ll.

The grene ys y mowe, and the bussche over throwe.
And the bagge yschake, thenne yt ys tyme Engelond to wake.

220. Prophecies affecting Richard II. **R.S.** CXV, 233. Date uncertain.   2 ll.

See the interesting and detailed account in the Annales Ricardi Secundi, Regis Angliae of the king's dependence on soothsayers and how he was Decipiebatur mempe cotidie per quosdam pseudo-prophetas.

Tunc opus est tauro proprio confidere stauro;   (and)
Ad gallum nomen tauri transibit, et omen.

221. Prophecy referring to Richard II's Original Name of "John." **R.S.** CXV, 237. Date uncertain.   1 l.

(This interesting legend is set forth in detail in the

prose context.)

Vix binis annis durabit pompa Johannis.

222. Richard the Redelesse. P. P. & S., I, 368. 1399. 857 ll.

And as I passid in my preiere there prestis were at
messe.

223. Gower's Tripartite Chronicle. P.P.&S., I, 417.
Date not ascertained.   1162 ll.

Ista tripartita sequitur quae mente perita.

224. Memorial Verses on the Reigns of Edward III and
Richard II. P. P. & S., I, 454. Date not ascertained. 120 ll.

Tertius Edwardus vivo genitore coronam.

F. FRANCE

225. On the Truce between England and France. P.P.&S.,
I, 300. Event, 1394.   56 ll.

Antre beauraym et le parc de Hedin,

G. SCOTLAND

226. The Battle of Otterburne. **R.** A.S.& B., I, sec. 2, III, p.
94. Event, August 9th, 1388.   280 ll.

Yt fell abowght the Lamasse tyde,
Whan husbondes wynne ther haye,

227. The Hontyng of the Cheviat. **R.** A.S.&B., I, sec. 2,
IV, p. 105. Date uncertain.   282 ll.

The Perse owt off Northombarlande,
And a vow to god mayd he,

H. ELEGIAC POEMS

228. On the Fate of Richard II. **R.S.** CXV, 332, n. 2. Date,
uncertain.   4 ll.

Note 2, p. 332: At the foot of this page (107), the following lines are written in, apparently, an almost contemporary hand.

Qui regis, intende, rotam fortunae cavete.
En Rex procerus, regum Richard recolendus;
Ecce! per auriloquos victus, cupidosque bilingues,
En cui servierat, fraude peremptus erat.

(The editor, H. T. Riley, does not suggest why the lines
occur in this place, and as they bear no relation to that part
of the text reproduced on p. 332, we may assume they were
inserted at random or because a blank offered in the Ms.
at the bottom of page 107.)

I· POEMS ON MISCELLANEOUS SUBJECTS.

229. On the Earthquake of 1382. **R.S.** XXXVI, III, 480.
Date, perhaps a later year.   2 ll.
   A. post Dunstanum, post tempus meridianum
   c. cuculum vixi, terraemotum, tibi dixi.
230. On the Times. P. P. & S., I, 270. 1388 (?)   232 ll.
   Syngun y wolde, but, alas!
   descendunt prospera grata;
   England sum tyme was
      regnorum gemma vocata;
231. Lak of Stedfastnesse. **C.** p. 630. 1389 (?)   28 ll.
   Som tyme this world was so stedfast and stable
232. On the Corruptions of the Age. P.P.&S., I, 346.
1396-7.   321 ll.
   Non excusatur qui verum non fateatur.
233. On the Vices of the Different Orders of Society. P.P.
& S., I, 356. 1396-7. (?)   103 ll.
   Heu! quia per crebras humus est vitiata tenebras,
234. The Baselard. S.& C., **W.C.**, IV, 84. Date uncertain.
                                                       32 ll.

      Prenegard, prenegard,
      Thus bere I myn baselard.
   Lestenit, lordynges, I zou beseke;   l. 1.
235. On the Decline of Virtue. S.&C., **P.S.**, XXIII, p. 96.
Date uncertain.   24 ll.
      God that sytteth in trinitie,
      Amend this world, if thi will it be.
   Vycyce be wyld, and vertues lame;   l. 1.
236 Penniless is Helpless. S.&C., **P.S.**, XXIII, 35. Date uncertain.   36 ll.
      Man upon mold, whatsoever thou be,
      I warn utterly thou getyst no degre,
237. Guile and Gold. S.&C., **W.C.**, IV, 13. Date uncertain.
                                                       20 ll.

      Now go gyle, gyle, gyle,
      Now go gile, gyle, go.
   Gyle and gold togedere arn met,   l. 1.
238. Power of the Purse. S.&C., **W.C.** IV, 14. Date uncertain.
                                                       16 ll.

      Syng we alle and sey we thus,
      Gramersy myn owyn purs.
   Quan I have in myn purs i-now,   l. 1.
239. Truth an Outlaw. S.& C., **W.C.**, IV, 19. Date uncertain.
                                                       24 ll.

God be with trewthe qwer he be,
I wolde he were in this cuntre.
A man that xuld of trewthe telle,   l. 1.
240.   Might of the Penny. S.& C., **W.C.**, IV, 75.   Date uncertain.   20 ll.

Go bet, peny, go bet, go,
For thou mat makyn bothe frynd and fo.
Peny is an hardy knyght;   l. 1.
241.   Syr Peny. **R.A.** II, 108.   Date, uncertain.   93 ll.
In erth there ys a lityll thyng,

J.   WELCOME TO HENRY IV.

242.   Complimentary Verses on King Henry IV. P. P. & S.,
II, 1, 3, and 15.   c. 1399.   100 ll.
    a.   Rex coeli Deus et Dominus, qui tempora solus
    b.   O recolende bone, pie rex Henrice, patrone,
    c.   Henrice quarti primus regni fuit annus
243.   Address of John Gower to Henry IV. P.P.& S., II, 4.
c. 1399.   7 ll. Lat.+385 ll. Eng.=   392 ll.
Electus Christi, pie rex Henrice, fuisti
O worthi noble kyng Henry the ferthe,   l. 8.

THE CHURCH

tions a treatise on subjects suggested by Peckham's "De Informatione Simplicium" and the five following constitutions: The writer was probably a monk, and the word Holme written on f. 123*b* may be his name. That he was a monk is suggested by his remarks on the duty of singing well and earnestly in the choir. "Hii sunt," he says, "qui psalmos corrumpunt nequiter almos.

Jangeler cum japer napper galper quoque dragger,
Momeler forskipper forrener sic overhipper.
Fragmina verborum Titivillus colligit horum."

253. On Careless Chanting. **R.A**. I, 90. Date uncertain.
                                                            2 ll.

Ecclesiae tres sunt, qui servitium male follunt;
Momylers, forscyppers, ovrelepers, non bene psallunt.

D. ATTACKS ON THE ECCLESIASTICAL COURTS.

254. A Satyre on the Consistory Courts. C.S. VI, p. 155. Edward I. (T. W.) (?)   90 ll.
Ne mai no lewed lued libben in londe

E. DEFENSES OF THE CHURCH.

255. Defensio Fratrum Mendicantium, per Joh. Peckham. **R.S.** LXXVII, III, cx. Ante 1292. (?) (Peckham died in that year.)   (c. 560 ll.)
O Christi vicarie, monarcha terrarum
Vir matris ecclesie, cella scriptuarum

POPULAR HEROES

A. FOR USE IN THE CHURCH SERVICE.

256. Lectionary for St. Kyneburg of Gloucester (and others). **R.S.** XXXIII, I, lxv & lxviii. Date of death, 1147. Translated, 1390. Date, uncertain.

Number of ll. not ascertained.
— — — — — — — — — — —l. 1.

Kyneburga generosa
  Multis effloruit virtutibus,
Cujus vita virtuosa
  Normam exhibuit claustralibus.

. . . .

Deo vero sit gloria,
    Qui dat de sua gratia
Nobis imitabilia
  Virginis exemplaria. Amen.

257. A Hymn for the Feasts after Christmas. (Including St. Thomas of Canterbury's Day). S. & C., **W.C.**, IV, p. 90. Date of death, 1170. Translated, 1220. Date, uncertain. 40 ll.

Non pudescit corpore,
Quod testatur hodic,
    Manna monumenti,
        dies.

258. Anthem of St. Thomas the Martyr. **E.E.T.S.** O. S., XLIX, 90. Post 1170. 10 ll.

Incipit Antiphona de sancto Thoma Martyre in Anglico
Haly thomas of heoueriche. l. 1
Alle apostles eueliche.
The Martyrs the vnderstonde.
Godfullyche in heore honde.
Selcuth dude vre dryhtin.
That he water wende to win.
Thu ert help in engelaunde.
Vre stephne vnderstonde.
Thu ert froure a-mong mon-kunne.
Help vs nv of vre sunne. Evovae.

259. Hymn to Simon de Montfort. C.S. VI., 124. Date of death, 1266. Date not ascertained. 13 ll.

Salve, Symon Montis-Fortis,
Totius flos militiae,
Duras poenas passus mortis,
Protector gentis Angliae.

260. The Office of St. Thomas of Lancaster. C.S. VI, 268.
Date of death, 1322. Date, uncertain.
A prose prayer of one sentence and 52 ll.

Ant. Gaude Thoma, ducum decus, lucerna Lancastriae,
Qui per necem imitaris Thomam Cantuariae;

. . . .

Interpella pro peccatis
nostris patrem gloriae,   l. 51.
Ut ascribat cum beatis
nos coelestis curiae. Amen.   l. 52.

B. MISCELLANEOUS POEMS.

261. A Carol for Saint Edmund's Day. **R**. A. S.&B., 1, 143.
Date of death, 870. Date, uncertain.   16 ll.
A newe song i wil begynne,
Of kyng Edmund that was so fre,
How he deyid without synne,
And bow[n]dyn his body was to a tre.

262. The Death of St. Thomas of Canterbury. S.& C., **W.C.**,
IV, 66. Died 1170. Translated, 1220. Date, uncertain.   36 ll.
A, a, a, a,
Nunc gaudet ecclesia.
Lestenytz, lordynges, bothe grete and smale, l. 1
I xal zou telyn a wonder tale,
How holycherche was brow[t] in bale,
Cum magna injuria.

263. A Carol for St. Thomas' Day. Songs and Carols. **P.S**.
XXIII, 51. Date of death, 1170. Translated, 1220. Date,
uncertain.   24 ll.
"Make we joy both more and lesse,
On the dey of sent Thomas
Pastor cesus in gregys medio,
Pacem emit cruorys precio.
As storys wryght and specyfy,   l. 1.
Sent Thomas, thorow Goddes sond,
Beyng a byschop of Canturbery,
Was martyrd for the ryght of Englond."